D0966554

THE ART AND SCIENCE OF AGGRESSIVE BASERUNNING

Cliff Petrak

Prentice-Hall, Inc.
Englewood Cliffs, New Jersey

© 1986 *by*

PARKER PUBLISHING COMPANY, INC.

West Nyack, N.Y.

All rights reserved. No part of this
book may be reproduced in any form or
by any means, without permission in
writing from the publisher.

Library of Congress Cataloging-in-Publication Data

Petrak, Cliff, 1942–
    The art and science of aggressive baserunning.

    Includes index.
    1. Base running (Baseball) 2. Baseball—Coaching.
I. Title.
GV868.P47   1986   796.357'27   85-30039

ISBN 0-13-047671-4

Printed in the United States of America

Acknowledgments

To photographer and friend, Martin Ritchey, for all his time, advice and supervision of our photo sessions.

To former Brother Rice High School players: Dan Harlan and Bob Ritchie who helped with the baserunning sequences, left-handed pitcher Mike Rukujzo, and right-handed pitcher Dave Spedale. Indeed, all of your time and assistance with the photography is truly appreciated.

To the Athletic Department of St. Xavier College, for the placement of their baseball facility at our disposal for the photo sessions.

To Randy Schwartz who gave of his time in producing the jacket photo.

Dedication

To Bill, who gave me my first mitt and took me to my first game

To Mom, who patiently heated and reheated countless meals while I played and coached

To George, who has been an exemplary coach and model for my own growth

To all my Crusader players, who have influenced my growth every bit as much as I have hopefully influenced theirs, and

To that college that may some day give me the opportunity to coach their ball club

Contents

How This Book Can Help You

The batter stares down the pitcher from his position at the plate. His immediate hope is to become a baserunner. His ultimate goal is to score a run. As simple as this sounds, the 360-foot circling of the bases represents perhaps the single, most important facet of the game of baseball outside of pitching. It's certainly the most exciting facet, as can be seen by the time accorded it on televised game highlights.

With the winning team defined as the one scoring the greater number of runs, each team must strive to outdo the other in its baserunning efforts to circle the bases. The winning team doesn't always have the better pitching, fielding, or hitting. It may not have the faster team either, but it must have demonstrated more efficient baserunning to win.

Of course, no one can discount the importance of hitting. It helps place runners on base. However, runs are not credited to batters who reach base, but only to those who are able to completely circle the bases.

The characteristics of good baserunning fall into three categories: attitude, strategy, and technique. However, only the technique category is of a physical nature. Technique answers the question, "How?" Strategy instead answers the questions, "What and when?" Once the strategy is determined, the technique is able to come into play. However, it is attitude that answers the most important question—"Why?" Why should the player bother to learn the how, what, and when? Attitude must precede strategy and technique in importance. Unless players become convinced of the enormous benefits of smart and aggressive baserunning, they will be reluctant to dedicate their efforts in that direction.

The way in which team members run the bases often ranges from pure timidity to utter foolhardiness. A happy medium should find players exhibiting a style of alertness mixed with confidence and aggressiveness and a touch of daring, yet falling short of reckless abandon. Attitude is a state of mind, however, and it must be instilled through the coach, if not through personal commitment. Baserunning is exciting and should be fun. The bases shouldn't be feared as kinds of remote outposts stationed long distances apart. Rather, they must be viewed as "our friends." Realistically, though, despite their friendliness, bases are still just nice places to visit. To paraphrase, "We wouldn't want to live there." Each base must then become the next launch spot from which to execute still more baserunning smarts. But such attitudes, as deeply rooted as they may and must become, still are not enough. It is just the beginning.

Coupled with this strong commitment to an aggressive attitude must be a high degree of smarts, especially in the area of strategy. This includes a working knowledge of the team's signal system as well as the baserunning rules of baseball. Players must learn to react quickly to a coach's signal, especially in multiple-runner situations where stunts and strategies require perfect timing and execution. Being able to play the percentages to the highest degree is a must. Under what circumstances should an extra base be attempted? . . .   A tag-up following a caught fly ball? . . .   A nonforce advancement on a ground ball? The answers to these and other similar questions must be within a split-second's reach for the aggressive baserunner.

Fortunately, whether it's strategy or any of the many techniques of baserunning that must be mastered, proper teaching and drilling can bring tremendous results. Unlike hitting, baserunning is a component of offensive baseball that is very teachable.

This book is for both the coach and player intent on incorporating smart and aggressive baserunning into their style of play. Every phase of the running game is discussed comprehensively, yet in a straightforward and down-to-earth manner. Every section is filled with facts, explanations, and directions. Intended for the serious student of the game, the book tries to get to the heart of each topic as quickly as possible. It refrains from indulging in chaff and needless banter.

Following the initial chapter on baserunning philosophy, a rules chapter is presented. It explains both the liberties and restrictions placed on every baserunner.

The art of sliding along with coverage of multiple-runner situations is covered in two other chapters. Numerous types of slides are discussed and analyzed in detail. Also discussed are each of the many possible stunts and strategies that present themselves in multiple-runner situations.

The actual trip around the bases is covered over five chapters, one of which spells out the general guidelines important at all the bases. The other four chapters each discuss the unique ninety feet of real estate between two particular bases along with the many singular scenarios encountered there.

The final chapter of drills and instructions is arranged in the same order as the first nine chapters. This way, the reader can quickly locate a suggested drill or instructional method to correspond to a particular baserunning topic presented in another part of the book.

The forms found in the Appendix are needed for use with some of the analyses and scouting drills mentioned and may be reproduced without permission.

In 1890, Edward J. Prindle was the first to recognize the importance of baserunning and write about it. It was just a small booklet, however, intended for beginners and entitled "The Art of Baserunning." In 1905 and again in 1948, new baserunning booklets emerged on the scene by different authors. But there was still no book on the subject for either the beginner or the serious student of the game. Many baseball instructional books written in recent years have included a chapter on baserunning. However, in such endeavors, authors have found it necessary to content themselves with a superficial treatment. To attempt to cover the full gamut of baserunning attitudes, techniques, strategies, and drills indeed requires a length and treatment that only a book could provide. It is hoped that this volume can and will help to fill that void that for so many years has been present in baseball-coaching literature.

Cliff Petrak

1

Aggressive Baserunning— The Mental Perspective

In studying the various techniques and strategies of baserunning, players must become enthusiastic about their purpose. There is so much to gain, but so much to learn, too. They must become convinced that what they are being taught will affect the play of the opposition. Even more important is the realization that the effect will be felt across all nine positions on the field. The defense's great awareness of the team's baserunning intentions will create in them considerable pressure. That kind of pressure leads to both mental and physical mistakes. The base runners must really believe this. If they do, their beliefs will lead to a strong team attitude toward aggressive and daring running.

Important, too, is the realization that such exciting baserunning is not reserved for just the one or two fastest players of the club. Even average-speed players can learn and contribute greatly when they are willing to dedicate their efforts toward a thorough study of baserunning.

Besides, speed by itself isn't enough. Knowledge of the team's signal system and strategies along with the incorporation of such abstract concepts as alertness, daring, and involvement are all very important. All too often these components don't get the

1

credit they deserve as vital characteristics of good base runners. But once their importance is realized by each player, a unifying team attitude will develop. From that point on, the team's baserunning alone will take it a long, long way.

THE INGREDIENTS OF SUCCESSFUL BASERUNNING

1 Average to better-than-average speed.
2 Aggressiveness without foolhardiness.
3 Confidence with no fear of failure.
4 Alertness and quick reflexes.
5 A deep involvement in the game.
6 Sliding ability.
7 A working knowledge of the fundamentals of good base-running techniques.
8 A thorough familiarization with the team's signal system and arm gestures of the coaches.

RECIPE FOR A WINNING BASERUNNING ATTITUDE

1 We will control the game with aggressive but intelligent baserunning.
2 We will be daring whenever the situation calls for such action.
3 We will accept our mistakes positively and turn them into constructive learning experiences.
4 We will be so aggressive that our runners won't have to be coaxed or encouraged by our coaches to run. Rather, we would like our coaches to hold up only those occasional runners who may tend to become overly aggressive to the point of foolhardiness.
5 We don't get credited with a run when one of our players becomes a base runner, only after he successfully circles those bases. Therefore, we won't sit back until our base runners have successfully completed their tasks.

BASERUNNING'S THREE KNOCKOUT PUNCHES

1 A strong feeling of awareness of our presence on the bases.
2 Pressure and more pressure brought on by that awareness.

3 Mistakes committed by the defense in their attempt to come up with perfect plays to stem our aggressiveness, knowing that any slip-up on their part will result in further advancement by our runners.

APPLYING PRESSURE AT EVERY DEFENSIVE POSITION

1 Pitcher: His control and effectiveness will be lessened when he becomes overly concerned with our aggressive runners. The more he tries to concentrate on our runners, the less he will be able to think about our hitters.

2 Catcher: He will reluctantly begin calling for more fast balls to better prepare himself for potential base-stealers. He may take some strikes away from the pitcher, too, by prematurely jumping up from his position in anticipation of possible steals.

3 Infielders: They will often be pulled out of position by both fake and real steals and will be forced through our pressure to come up with quick and flawless fielding and throwing. This feeling of tightness will often bring on errors.

4 Outfielders: Through our aggressiveness, they will sometimes take their eyes off the ball as they try to keep our runners in sight. They will also be forced to hurry their throws, thus increasing the odds of a bad throw.

★★

Drills and methods of instruction for Chapter 1 may be found on page 151.

★★

2

Running by the Rules

When reviewing baserunning guidelines, it must be remembered that not all represent some special heads-up, aggressive strategy of thought and motion. Much baserunning is no more than simple compliance with the rules of the game. To anyone having played a few years, most of these rules have become second-nature and hardly need mentioning. Others, though, require more thought and do indeed lead to strategic follow-up moves that produce runs and win ball games.

Those rules most important to the base runner are listed here and, in some cases, a strategic suggestion that might otherwise go unthought of follows. The first group of rules applies to the batter-runner. The second group deals with all the other runners. A few will be discussed again in later chapters. Wherever differences in the rules exist on different levels of organized ball, comments are made to that effect.

A knowledge of these rules is essential to the serious-minded ballplayer intent on becoming an adept base runner.

THE BATTER-RUNNER AND THE RULES

On a walk, the batter must go directly to first base. Otherwise, he can be called out if he first heads toward the dugout (especially the third-base dugout) for a jacket, a cap, or anything else. Instead, the batter should go directly to first and only then, if necessary, call for time to handle any of these other matters.

While sprinting to first on a walk certainly demonstrates hustle, the runner must slow down as he nears the base. On a walk, the runner is not accorded the luxury of overrunning first base as he does when trying to beat a throw there.

With two outs (whether first base is occupied or not), the batter-runner may run to first base on a dropped third strike or on a third strike clearly trapped by the catcher. Either the batter-runner or the first-base bag must be tagged by the defense for the out. The rule doesn't apply with less than two outs. The reason is clear. By intentionally dropping a third strike, the catcher could easily execute a 2-6-3 double play if first base was occupied. In this situation, it is not a bad idea for the batter sometimes to take off for first base anyway. Occasionally, the catcher, either sleeping or unaware of the rule, will throw the ball to first. Even though the batter would still be ruled out, another runner might be able to advance. Besides the possibility of an overthrow into right field, an advance might result on the throw itself. Of course, if the catcher smartly holds the ball, nothing would be lost beyond the obvious strikeout.

The batter-runner may not interfere with a defensive player such as the pitcher, catcher, or first baseman. Such interference might occur as the defensive player tries to handle a fair or foul pop-up, a ground ball, or a bunt near the baseline. However, the batter-runner is allowed to run inside or outside the baseline to avoid the interference.

Once the batter is on his way to first, he may not contact his own hit ball either intentionally or unintentionally. Being hit by such a ball while still in the batters' box merely results in a dead ball.

While running the bases, a runner may not remove his helmet. If such removal is judged intentional, the runner would be called out. This rule exists in most amateur leagues.

In many leagues, the throwing of a helmet constitutes grounds for an ejection. It makes no difference whether the reason be in disgust at the umpire's call or disgust at the player's own performance. The penalty remains the same in both cases for this act of unsportsmanship.

Proper umpiring technique dictates that the call "Foul ball" be shouted out while "Fair ball" be only indicated. Therefore, on a hot shot hit down the third-base line, the batter should never wait to hear a "Fair ball" call. He will never hear one. He will hear only "Foul ball" when that's the case.

When any ball is fielded near the baseline to first, the batter-runner must avoid interference. To do this, he is expected to run the final 45 feet within the rectangular-lined area whose dimensions are 45 feet by 3 feet. This is written into the rules to prevent interference with a throw to first. A call would be made against the batter-runner if he were outside that area and the resulting throw to first went astray. Whether or not the ball were to hit the batter-runner would be irrelevant. The runner could, however, go wide of these guidelines to avoid contact with a fielder who is handling a hit ball such as a pop-up as mentioned earlier. In trying to avoid a tag, the batter-runner may run no more than 3 feet from a direct line to the next base.

Some plays require the pitcher to run toward first base to take a throw from the first baseman following a ground ball. The pitcher will try to remain in fair territory and run parallel to the baseline to avoid a collision. The collisions that do occur are usually ruled as incidental contact, especially if the pitcher has the ball or is in the process of receiving the throw. However, if this contact is made before the toss is made, an obstruction call could be made in favor of the runner. For this reason, the runner may wish to produce some contact if the pitcher does penetrate the 45-foot line.

In trying to beat a throw to first, the batter-runner may, of course, overrun the bag. He may even turn toward second as he eventually stops and begins his return to the bag. However, he is not allowed to feint even one step in the direction of second. Such movement places the runner in jeopardy of being tagged out. Therefore, he must be sure to return directly to first along the first-base line or very close to it.

RUNNERS ON BASE AND THE RULES

If, after he has advanced to the next base, a fly ball is caught with less than two out, the runner must first retouch that base before returning to the original base. Failure to retouch would find that runner being called out at the conclusion of the play if high school rules were in effect. Professional rules would require an appeal play to be made by the defense.

When two runners find themselves perched on the same base, it is the front runner who is entitled to the base. Even if both runners were tagged, the back runner would be the one declared out. Embarrassing situations have found unknowing base runners both stepping off the base after having been tagged. By simply retagging the front runner after he has stepped off the base, the defense produces a double play. A confused runner should stay in contact with the base until told by the umpire that he is out and should vacate the bag.

A runner who finds himself in a rundown may be able to get obstruction called on a defensive player. The baseline belongs to the runner. Any defensive player without the ball and not in the process of receiving the ball must stay clear of the runner. Therefore, the runner should look for this opportunity for contact with any player in the base path. He should remain watchful for the fielder who has just thrown the ball but who remains planted and fails to move for the runner.

The runner is out when he interferes with a fielder attempting to make a play on a batted ball. The same is true when he intentionally interferes with a thrown ball. In fact, the umpire could rule a double play in this situation. If he felt that the interference prevented a possible double play, such a call would be made.

While a runner may not steal on a foul ball, he may do so on a foul tip because the ball remains alive. If the ball comes directly into the catcher's mitt from its contact with the bat, it is not considered a foul ball but a foul tip. Runners arriving at second safely should never allow the defense to make them believe that the ball was hit foul. If unsure, the runner should check with the umpire before stepping off.

The runner may not deviate more than 3 feet in either direction from a direct line between bases to avoid a tag.

In most amateur leagues, runners are not allowed to plow into a fielder in an attempt to dislodge the ball on a tag play. This applies when the fielder receives the throw in plenty of time and is waiting for the runner on a sure out play. In this situation, the runner must either slide, give himself up, or reverse and get into a rundown.

A runner may try to disrupt the pivot man on an attempted double play. Both professional and amateur rules stipulate that the runner may not leave the base path to such a distance that some form of contact could not have been maintained with the bag. In addition, the runner may not deliberately interfere with the throw. However, the rules differ on what constitutes a legal slide. In professional ball, it seems as if the sky's the limit, the runner being permitted his choice of slide. But, in an attempt to stem injuries, most amateur rules restrict runners to the usual feet-first and head-first slides. Roll slides, football roll blocks, and leg slashing are all strictly forbidden. Malicious or flagrant contact with such illegal slides results in ejection. Leaving the baseline with either a legal or illegal slide to upset the pivot man constitutes interference. The runner is called out and a double play could be called if it was judged that a second out was prevented.

Regardless of the base involved, a runner must always advance to the next base in a force situation if the play finds the winning run coming across the plate with two outs. Failure to do so could result in the third out being called in one of two ways. In professional ball, the defensive team could make an appeal at the base that wasn't tagged. In high school rules, the umpire would call an automatic out in lieu of the now nonexistent appeal play.

When attempting to score with two outs, the runner should run hard so as to score before a third out may be recorded at another base. This sometimes occurs following a hit to the outfield when the throw-in toward the plate is cut off and relayed to another base. If the tag there is made before the earlier runner has crossed the plate, the run is disallowed and the inning is over.

A runner is out if he is hit by a batted ball before it has passed a fielder. However, an exception does exist. A runner hit by a pop-up while standing on a base when the infield-fly rule is in effect is not out. Otherwise, the runner is not protected from an "out" call even if he is in contact with a base when hit.

The infield-fly rule needs some clarification. The rule was instituted to eliminate the possibility of setting up an easy double play over which the offense would have little control. The rule applies to fair fly balls hit with less than two outs and with runners on first and second or with the bases loaded. The fly ball must be one judged to be a reasonably easy ball to catch by an infielder. The rule does not apply to popped-up bunts or line drives. On the infield-fly-rule call, the ball must eventually come down in fair territory or the call is disregarded. The batter is automatically out whether or not the ball is caught. The runners may advance at their own risk. Of course, if the ball is dropped, no tag up is necessary. Any back runner should return to his base in anticipation of a catch.

However, the lead runner should stray off his base as far as he safely can if he feels that the infielder may have problems with the fly. If the ball is dropped, the runner will have an edge if he decides to try an advance. On the other hand, if the lead runner feels that the catch will be easy, then it would be wiser to prepare instead to tag-up and perhaps fake a break. It might just draw a wild throw.

A runner may not pass another runner who has not yet been put out on the bases. This sometimes occurs when, on a long fly, a runner at first will consider tagging up while the batter-runner, hoping that the ball will drop and thinking of extra bases, will run past the front runner. There also is the chance of this happening on any long drive that produces an extra-base hit. The preceding runner(s) might decide to hold momentarily to see if there is a chance of the ball's being caught. In the meantime, the careless batter-runner passes by and is called out.

★★★

Drills and methods of instruction for Chapter 2 may be found on pages 151–52.

★★★

3

The Mechanics and Strategy of Sliding

In no way can a ballplayer become a truly great base runner without mastering the ability to slide. This is a must! Runners are constantly being told to take the extra base whenever possible. But the runner must realize, too, that such aggressive running will bring with it numerous close plays at all the bases. The good slide, then, takes on an added importance.

Depending on the situation, a good slide can accomplish any one of a number of desired results: the breakup of a double play, the presentation of a small target and possibly the avoidance of a tag, the avoidance of overrunning a base, or the ability to pop up quickly after a slide for the purpose of continuing on to the next base.

Whatever its purpose, the slide must be performed with confidence; not a confidence that every slide will result in a safe call, but a confidence that the slide will be performed aggressively and correctly—most important, that the slide will be executed in a relaxed state without any fear of injury.

To accomplish such lofty goals obviously requires much practice. While teams spend days and weeks on other phases of the

game, so often the practice of proper sliding techniques is neglected. Often this neglect comes about from a fear that an injury
could occur during practice. However, if the runner takes the
time to study the mechanics of a particular slide before actually
trying it in practice, he will be helped into achieving the necessary
relaxed state. Helping to reduce any chance of injury is the use of
a number of sliding aids and safeguards, including proper dress
and a physically well-suited practice area.

It really isn't necessary to master all of the slides described in
this chapter. A couple will suffice for just about every situation
that will confront a runner. What is really important, though, is
that the runner come to look upon an anticipated slide as something that will be fun! It will be enjoyable because the runner's
knowledge of its proper execution will assure him that the slide
will be injury-free, will be aesthetically pleasing to view, and will
stand a great chance of accomplishing its purpose.

DEFINITION AND PURPOSE

Sliding is the art of controlled falling from a running position.
While it doesn't get the runner to the next base any sooner, it
greatly reduces the target on a tag play, prevents overrunning the
base, and will upset or hinder the pivot man on an attempted double play.

SLIDING AIDS AND SAFEGUARDS

1   Practice sliding techniques with (a) loose bases, (b) gym shoes or
    in socks, and (c) on soft ground, wetted grass, or in a sliding pit.

2   Sliding pads (or even gym shorts) will protect the lower back-
    side and hips.

3   Sanitary socks will help prevent needless abrasions by covering
    the legs and the areas left exposed by the tube socks.

4   Knee or ankle bandage wraps can aid those ballplayers with a
    history of injuries in these areas.

5   While most leagues require the wearing of a helmet while run-
    ning the bases, this piece of safety equipment should also be
    worn while practicing sliding if live throws are involved. The

runner should also try to slide in the direction that will keep his face away from the throw.

6   Place dirt in each hand to form two filled fists. This can help to prevent finger injuries (especially jams) and can act as a reminder to keep the hands up as the slide is executed.

GENERAL REMINDERS AND GUIDELINES

The decision to slide into first base must be solely that of the runner's. To try to react to a "Slide!" command by the first-base coach is inviting trouble. The runner instead should anticipate a slide whenever he sees the first baseman moving off the bag and to the home-plate side to take a high throw. This play requires a sweeping tag by the fielder. A low slide (head-first or feet-first) could avoid the tag.

At second base, the runner is pretty much on his own although the third-base coach may still be heard calling out instructions as to whether the runner should slide or come in standing. There are two important rules to remember here as guidelines:

1   On any close play, slide and slide aggressively. If in doubt that a play is being made, slide anyway.

2   The runner's mind must never get changed once the decision to slide has been made. This is the greatest cause of sliding injuries. A last second change of plans will often result in spikes getting caught since sufficient room does not remain to extend the leg. As a result, the leg and spike stick while the rest of the body continues to attempt to go through with its portion of the slide. The ankle bones and ligaments are most vulnerable here.

Approaching third, the runner looks and listens for the appropriate signal from the third-base coach and places full confidence in his decision. He must try to be aware of the side of the base from which the throw is coming. Obviously, he must slide to the opposite side. Again, the third-base coach may indicate this. It is important, though, that this decision be made no less than 20 feet from the bag.

It is the duty of the on-deck hitter to give the slide or stand-up gesture to a runner coming in from third. Once the runner passes the third-base coach, that runner must pick up the on-deck hitter for instructions. Otherwise, anything else he might hear from the coach could be intended for a following runner.

With any slide on a tag play, make as little contact as possible with the bag so as to present a small target as well as less opportunity for an injury.

How much distance must be allowed for the slide will depend on the speed of the runner, his height, field conditions, and the type of slide to be used. Usually, for a feet-first slide, 1 to 1 ½ body lengths or 5 to 10 feet is about right.

With any feet-first type of slide, the back of the shoulders should be parallel to the ground with the arms and hands back.

SLIDES: TYPES, EXECUTION, AND STRATEGY

The Head-First Slide (Fig. 3-1)

This is a very aggressive type of slide that seems more often than not to gain the close call of the umpire. It is not to be used when a force play is involved or when the base is being blocked.

So as to provide the smallest possible tag area, the slide should be executed to the outside of the bag with the left hand grabbing out for just a corner of the base.

The knees and hands should hit the ground simultaneously with the chest very close behind. This is important since to do it otherwise will result in a painful, belly-flop fall.

Because the runner's upper body is already leaning forward, no reversal of the body angle becomes necessary to go into the slide. For this reason, many feel that the head-first slide gets the runner to the base quicker than does any variation of a feet-first slide.

Figure 3-1   Head-First Slide—The hands and knees make contact with the ground simultaneously as the slide is made to the outside of the base.

(Figure 3-1 continued)

The Feet-First Slide (Fig. 3-2)

The runner may use this slide to beat a throw on a force play. Because no tag is involved, he slides directly into the bag with both legs extended.

While the runner may begin his slide to either the left or right side, it is the hip and the back of the leg that will absorb the friction of the contact. The runner should bear in mind the side from which the throw will be coming so as to be turned the other way.

When going down, the runner must be sure not to go up immediately as in some sort of a jump. This only causes pain and "strawberries." Sliding should be fun. In this slide, it is one buttock or the other that absorbs the fall with the hip and the side.

Figure 3-2   Feet-First Slide—The base is approached directly since no tag is involved on a force play. Contact is absorbed by the back of the upper leg and hip.

(Figure 3-2 continued)

The Hook Slide (Fig. 3-3)

Used in avoiding tags, this slide is also known as a "fadeaway slide." While it's also sometimes called the "93-foot slide," this nickname is really not deserved if proper techniques are employed. The advantage of the hook slide lies in the very small tag area exposed to the infielder. With body flat and away from the base and with only about 6 inches of foot contacting the base, the advantage is obvious.

Most runners have a preference for hooking left or right. For most runners, it is the hook to the right or outside of the base which works best for throws coming from the inside of the diamond. Throws from the outfielders, however, usually call for hook slides to the inside or left side of the base. Therefore, both should be practiced and perfected.

Assuming the hook slide is to the left side, the technique is as follows: The left buttock takes most of the hit as the runner goes down off his collapsing left leg. Both legs are extended and kept a

Figure 3-3 Hook Slide—Only about three inches of target are provided for the infielder. The legs split into a hook position only after the base-tagging leg has contacted the base.

(Figure 3-3 continued)

bit bent, but also with the feet off the ground sufficiently to prevent any spikes from catching. It is very important to refrain from immediately going into the hook position. This improper technique of quickly bending the right leg before it has contacted the base requires the runner to travel about another 3 feet, thus the dubious nickname of the "93-foot slide."

When executed properly, the toes of an arched and pointed right foot will contact the left corner of the bag. The left leg remains slightly bent and the left foot off the ground by a couple of inches to avoid spike-catching. The right leg, bent slightly more than the left, will be carried forward by momentum along with the rest of the body, producing the desired hook.

While the runner may find himself somewhat beyond the base, none of the slide will have gone wasted. The initial contact will have come 3 feet earlier. In sliding primarily on the left buttock and hip, no problem should exist in keeping the right hand and elbow up. However, some effort will have to be made to keep the left elbow off the ground along with the left hand.

A dirt-filled fist can help as a reminder as the runner tries to go through his slide without losing the dirt. On a very hard field, though, the runner may wish to absorb part of the contact with his palm-down, left hand. The eyes, aided by a slightly bent neck, should remain on the base.

In hooking to the right side, everything is just the opposite. The shock of the slide will fall on the right buttock as the take-off is made off the collapsing right leg.

The Back-Door Hook Slide

When the runner feels himself to be a sure out on a tag play, he may wish to employ this variation of the hook slide. It is used to decoy the infielder into thinking that the standard hook slide is coming. Instead, the runner slides to the outside and beyond the base, reaching out for the back of the base with the *outside* hand at the last possible moment. Reaching with this outside hand will require a turn toward the bag, but will also require the runner to pull the left arm and hand in toward the body as far as possible from the reach of the infielder. Of course, the hooking of the base with the foot never takes place since both legs remain extended through the slide. The idea is for the runner to make the infielder look for the hooking foot. Instead, it's his outside hand that makes contact with the base, not at the front end but at the base's backside.

Another variation of the back-door slide incorporates the partial use of the bent-leg slide. It will be explained later in this chapter following a discussion of the standard bent-leg slide.

The Take-Out Slide (Fig. 3-4)

Intended to break up a double-play attempt, this slide is the amateur player's answer to the roll slide, which is allowed in most professional leagues, but not in amateur ball.

To execute the take-out slide, the runner begins his slide with his body at a slight angle to the bag and with both legs extended. The hands and arms remain up after the body hits the ground in order to protect the face and upper body from any serious contact with the legs of the pivot man.

For players in professional leagues which allow the roll slide, the take-out slide is quickly followed by a forward roll into the legs of the pivot man in hopes of upsetting his balance.

Neither the take-out slide nor the roll slide should be intended to harm or injure in the process of being executed. The idea is merely to prevent the pivot man from completing his necessary weight transfer to his front leg as he makes the throw. Sliding or rolling into this leg often accomplishes the purpose.

Rules prohibit the runner from raising his hands while still in an upright position for the purpose of interfering with the throw. In addition, he is not allowed to follow the pivot man so far out of the base path that he would lose contact with the base.

Some guesswork will be necessary to determine the path that the pivot man will take to get off his throw. However, watching the opposition work on their double plays during infield practice can be a big help, especially in the case of the second baseman.

Figure 3-4   The Take-Out Slide—The slide is executed with the body
at a slight angle to the bag, both legs extended and arms and hands up.

(Figure 3-4 continued)

The Bent-Leg Slide (Fig. 3-5)

Very safe, popular, practical, and versatile, this slide's many purposes include: (1) the prevention of overrunning and oversliding a base; (2) a quick pop-up back to the feet of a runner who may have already decided to slide but who has realized that either no play is being made on him or that a wild throw will now allow him to advance farther; (3) a variation for the purpose of upsetting the pivot man on a double-play attempt; (4) a variation which acts like the previously discussed back door slide to avoid a tag; and (5) its use (similar to the hook-slide variation) to avoid the tag of a fielder who appears to have the runner beaten.

The slide should begin no more than 9 to 10 feet from the bag. The takeoff can come off either leg, but sliding on a tucked-under left leg will place the runner in the direction of the next base as opposed to the outfield side. However, coming up out of a right-leg, bent-leg slide facing away from the next base is not as important as the comfort and confidence of a slide well done. With practice, though, both sides can be mastered.

To execute this slide, decide which leg will be bent. Let's assume a left-leg, bent-leg slide will be made. Then, with the favored left leg bent, the other leg is extended and only very slightly bent to avoid a knee injury. The toes are about 4 inches off the ground to prevent the spikes from catching. With shoulders square, the upper body follows in a half-sitting or sit-up position. To cushion the slide and to distribute the weight evenly, the runner lays back with his hands in the air in front of him as if he's holding on with both hands to a vertical steering wheel. As the upper body starts to go down, the head should stay back to prevent the knee of the bent leg from hitting the ground first. The underside of the bent leg and thigh should absorb most of the weight of the fall. This is important if "strawberries" are to be held to a minimum.

Running with dirt held in a closed fist will also help to minimize needless finger jams and will also act as a reminder to keep the hands up. Banged-up elbows and scraped and bruised hands will also be greatly reduced. The hands, arms, and elbows must stay up! Remember, too, that the foot of the extended leg makes the initial contact with the base.

Figure 3-5 Bent Leg Slide—The shoulders remain squared while the extended leg is elevated about four inches to prevent the spikes from catching.

(Figure 3-5 continued)

The Pop-Up Variation of the Bent-Leg Slide (Fig. 3-6)

This pop-up variation is used for the purpose of quickly coming up out of the normal bent-leg slide. It occurs when the runner has already committed himself to a slide. But seeing an opportunity to continue on to the next base, the runner wishes to get back to his feet as quickly and efficiently as possible. To convert a bent-leg slide into this variation, merely raise the head to a more upright position and lean forward, also keeping the arms up. Body momentum will do the rest to bring the runner quickly into a standing position.

    If the runner knows from the start that this is to be a pop-up slide, he should never allow his upper body and head to droop back very far. This only makes it more difficult to bring about the quick pop-up. However, once popped up and on the base, the runner is ready to go on to the next base. Realize, then, the advantage of popping up on the right leg rather than the left. The latter method requires an additional crossover step to get pointed in the direction of the next base.

Figure 3-6 Bent Leg Pop-Up Slide—Momentum coupled with an upper body lean bring the runner into a standing position. Bending the left leg saves one step in advancing to the next base.

(Figure 3-6 continued)

The Double-Play Take-Out Variation of the Bent-Leg Slide (Fig. 3-7)

This is the second of the two recommended slides for upsetting the pivot man in a double-play situation. The first method was the earlier discussed roll slide.

This double-play take-out variation is still basically the bent-leg slide, but most definitely is a hard slide. On landing the runner should lean somewhat toward the side of the bent leg. The runner should hook the foot of the pivot man's striding leg. However, whether he hooks it or not, he must stay up some (without popping up) so as to get the pivot man into the air and off balance.

The Hook Variation of the Bent-Leg Slide

Like the normal hook slide, the purpose of this bent-leg hook variation is to avoid a tag even though it might appear that a throw will have the runner beaten. A regular hook slide will find the runner sliding to the outside of the bag and then hooking it with an outstretched foot. This variation has the runner hooking the bag with an outstretched arm. Beginning the slide about 8 to 10 feet from the base, the runner keys on a point about a full arm's length from the bag. With the upper torso back to prevent a high tag on the shoulder, the runner reaches with his closer hand for the front corner of the base. There is less chance of the hand losing contact as there would be with the foot. Also, with the weight more evenly distributed than with the more traditional hook, the appearance of "strawberries" is far less likely.

The Back-Door Hook Variation of the Bent-Leg Slide

Referred to earlier, this bent-leg slide variation is used when all seems lost to the runner who can see the fielder waiting for him with the ball. The technique begins in the very same way as the bent-leg slide with the hook variation except for one point. Just when the fielder is about to tag the outstretched arm of the runner, the base runner quickly pulls the arm back in toward his body. As his body then slides by the base, the runner makes a cat-like grab for the back end of the base with the *right* hand. Again,

Figure 3-7   Bent Leg "Double Play Take Out" Slide—Performed aggressively, this slide has the runner hopefully trying to hook the stride leg of the pivot man. The upper body and arms remain up. The player leans toward the side of the bent leg.

(Figure 3-7 continued)

the upper body must stay low to avoid a high shoulder or head tag and to enable the runner a chance to come in by way of the "back door."

Finally, there is one last situation in which the runner may wish to employ this slide with another slight variation. At first base, it would be the situation where the first baseman goes high off the base to take a throw to the home-plate side. Also, at home plate, it would be the familiar case of the catcher doing a good job of blocking the plate, but stationed up the baseline a bit, leaving the back part unprotected. In both situations, the runner employs the standard bent-leg slide, staying low but also sliding wide of the bag and tag. In this variation, he does not offer his hand out as he goes by the fielder, nor does he even fake with his arm. Instead, he keeps his left arm in close to the body until he is past the fielder when he hopes he will have arrived at the base without having been tagged. Remember, in both cases the fielder is up the line when trying to apply the tag. Sliding past the fielder will not mean sliding past the base, too. However, depending on just how wide of the baseline the slide was made will foretell whether the runner will be able to reach for and tag the base with his left hand or with a right-handed turning grab.

★★

Drills and methods of instruction for Chapter 3 may be found on pages 152–53.

★★

4

What Every Base Runner Should Know

There are some tenets of good baserunning that can't be singled out for use between two particular bases only. Instead, they must be applied at every base. There are guidelines, for instance, that every runner is encouraged to follow while perched on a base and still others that must be remembered while in a leadoff. A few ideas also apply to all runners as they begin their advance to the next base as a ball is hit. All of them in one way or another are more examples of those important characteristics of good baserunning at work: aggressiveness, daring, alertness, signal knowledge, and deep involvement in the game.

Although Chapter 9 deals with specific multiple-runner situations, some strategic guidelines will be found here as well. They should be used to guide the actions of multiple runners, regardless of the bases they occupy.

STANDING ON A BASE

Before every pitch, the runner looks to the coach for a sign. If doubt exists, the runner calls for time rather than trying to guess. However, this means that an offensive conference is being used unnecessarily. Ideally, a signal system should exist for just this situation. Such a prearranged signal from the runner to the coach asks the coach to repeat the signal.

Every runner's mind should be like a computer stored with vital information. He should know the score, inning, number of outs, other runners on base, and the positioning of the infielders and outfielders along with the strength of their arms. He should also be fully aware of the meaning and execution of the various signals that may be flashed his way.

Gambling on the bases is aggressive baserunning when ahead in the score. However, discretion is the characteristic of a good base runner when his team is trailing, especially late in the game.

A runner never begins his leadoff if the pitcher's foot isn't on the rubber, much less if he is off the mound.

IN THE PRIMARY OR SECONDARY LEADOFF

With every pitch, anticipate a passed ball or wild pitch. Be ready to jump upon such a gift opportunity. Anticipation is the key word.

In the absence of a batted ball, wild pitch, or passed ball, the runner must hustle back quickly to the bag. He shouldn't get caught sleeping by underestimating the strength of the catcher's arm or his willingness to throw to the bag in an attempted pickoff.

Be watchful for a bad throw back to the pitcher from the catcher. Notice which infielder, if any, guards against such an overthrow after every pitch.

The runner must freeze in his tracks whenever a line drive is seen coming off a bat with less than two out unless it can be determined whether the ball will be caught or not. Double plays resulting from this action should be the exception, not the rule.

Whenever the pitcher carelessly goes into a full windup, the runner should always be ready to advance to the next base (other than home).

A runner must go on a hit-and-run play, but following a normal steal sign, he should not go through with the steal if he falters on his first step or is fooled by a pitcher's motion. There is no sense in chalking up an easy out for the opposition just to be able to say that the signal given was seen and executed.

ADVANCING TO THE NEXT BASE

On pop-ups and fly balls with two outs, always run at full speed unless it is obvious that the ball won't be caught. In case the ball is dropped, have in mind that base which would appear easiest to reach. The runner must not allow himself to get caught between two bases in this situation. When such a ball is dropped, the offense should gain, not the defense.

When tagging up after a catch, the base runner can give himself some momentum by shifting his weight low just before the catch. This will provide him with extra thrust in his pushoff toward the next base.

Be sure that an out call by the umpire has been heard or that a hit ball has been ruled foul before stepping off a base to which an advance has just been made.

When thinking of possibly advancing beyond the base to which he is headed, the runner must angle out as the base is approached. This will allow for a sharper turn and a shorter distance to the next base. The execution of this turn is identical to the turn at first base which will be discussed in the next chapter.

Round all bases by hitting the inside corner of the bag with the left foot if possible. Lean hard to the inside of the diamond for the best pushoff possible. Be sure, though, not to break stride for this purpose. It's better to hit the base with the right foot in stride than to break stride for the sole purpose of hitting it with the favored left foot.

GENERAL BASERUNNING GUIDELINES
FOR MULTIPLE-RUNNER SITUATIONS

- After crossing the plate, remove any bat still remaining in the home-plate area and remain there to coach any oncoming runner.
- With two outs and a 3-2 count on the batter, be absolutely certain that the pitcher is going to the plate with the ball before breaking to the next base.
- Be constantly aware of the intentions of any front runner. Avoid the embarrassing situation of tagging up and advancing

after a fly ball has been hit only to find that the lead runner has decided to remain at his base. This can also occur following a wild pitch or passed ball.

- A hitter who has just singled and who is certain that a throw to the plate intended to cut down another runner is over the cut man's head, should advance to the next base if it is unoccupied. A runner starting out at first base might take third in this situation, but he must be more cautious since a follow-up throw by the catcher need only travel 90 feet and not 127 as it must to second.

- With less than two outs, the back (free) runner in a rundown should get to the next base if at all possible, but he should give the front (caught) runner a base to return to with two outs. However, when two runners find themselves on the same base, the back runner is the one who should vacate the base and try to return to the previous base since he is the one who will be ruled out if both are tagged. It is extremely important for this back runner to try to return to the previous base *only after* the front runner has arrived at the same base as the back runner. Otherwise, a double play could become a distinct possibility.

- If the back runner is caught in a rundown, the free front runner may be able to catch the defense napping and advance a base, which could mean scoring. If the defense does quickly switch its attention to the lead runner and trap him, the lead runner's responsibility is to stall so that the back runner can move up at least one base. In this way, the offense can salvage one runner still in scoring position. One stall tactic by which a runner can eat up a second or two is to fall down in the basepath, necessitating the defensive player to bend over to make the tag and maybe stumble in the process. Another tactic is to run out of the base path. This might be done by a runner who was certain of being tagged out. Although the umpire would call out a runner who left the baseline by more than 3 feet to avoid a tag, often the defensive player will continue to follow after him to apply the tag.

- A lead runner who finds himself about to be a sure out (with less than two outs) at third or home on a tag play should stop short of the base and get in a rundown. This stalling maneuver will give the back runner a chance to move up a base.

- With two outs, a runner who finds himself rounding third and headed for home with no play to be made on him must still run hard. He must remember that a play might be in the process of being made on another runner. If such runner is called out before the lead runner crosses the plate, the run is nullified. For this reason, the lead runner must sprint home all the way.

★★

Drills and methods of instruction for Chapter 4 may be found on pages 153–54.

★★

5

From the Dugout to First

To win, a team must score runs. To score runs, a team must produce runners, and to do that, those runners must first get on base safely. That means successfully acquiring that first 90 feet of real estate. Yet, when baserunning is discussed, those first 90 feet are either glossed over superficially or neglected entirely. This is because too many feel that the runner really has little in his bag of tricks to influence the outcome of this short jaunt other than just running as fast as possible. That kind of thinking makes for some very dull baserunning and will be sure to reduce run production and on-base percentages.

Smart base runners learn early that their duties begin not when they arrive at first, but back in the dugout before they even come to bat. From there, those obligations increase at a fast pace as the ballplayer moves to the on-deck circle, to the batters' box, and finally, out of that box as the ball is hit. There is a proper and efficient way for getting out of the box and for getting down the line quickly, too, regardless of the quickness of the runner. His speed can and must be maximized if he is going to be a top-notch base runner.

As the runner nears first, he must have read the situation correctly, partly on his own and partly through the help of the first-

41

base coach. He knows whether he will be running through the bag or taking a turn, and there certainly is a correct way of doing each. Just rounding a base takes a lot of thought, study, and practice if it's to be done in the most efficient manner.

Finally, in continuing to follow a philosophy of aggressive and daring baserunning, the runner who knows he has first must be thinking of the possibility of going to second even before he rounds the bag. He must be aware of the conditions that would warrant such a try just as well as those that would prohibit a try for the extra base.

This chapter, then, will help to teach young and old alike how best to "run away from home."

IN THE DUGOUT

Review the team signal system as well as the meaning of the various arm gestures of the base coaches for rounding a base, sliding, taking a turn, and so forth.

Watch for special pickoff plays, the frequency of pickoff attempts, the usual depth of the infielders, and the types of pickoff moves employed by the pitcher. Tip-offs on the pitcher's move to first are especially important to determine before arriving at first later in the game. The team that has the first-base dugout has an advantage in determining such tip-offs due to the angle created between the pitcher and dugout. Those watching for the pitcher's pick-off characteristics should position themselves near the first-base end of the dugout.

IN THE ON-DECK CIRCLE

After a ball has been hit that will bring one or more runners across the plate, the next hitter should position himself behind home plate out of the way of the catcher and umpire. Yet, he must remain in line with third base where advancing runners on the line can see him clearly. He should also move any loose equipment out of the way. Thus, any runner(s) trying to score can be given the arm signal to slide or come in standing.

IN THE BATTERS' BOX

The batter must be ready to advise quickly any runner on third following a pitch that gets away from the catcher.

A runner on second who has successfully read the catcher's signals may try to relay them to the batter, who must be alert to this possibility. Such a relay signal system should be a part of a team's overall signal system.

If any uneven or lumpy area which could cost a step is noticed on the first-base side of home plate, the batter should smooth it out before stepping in to hit.

GETTING OUT OF THE BATTERS' BOX

Whether the batter be left- or right-handed, his first step out of the box should be made with his rear foot. This would be the right foot for the right-handed batter and the left foot for the left-handed batter. When this is not happening, it is usually the result of a poor weight distribution, hitting off the heels, or swinging too hard.

On a questionable ball hit down the third-base line, the batter should begin running immediately. He doesn't wait for an umpire's call. If it is ruled a fair ball, the umpire wouldn't make a verbal call anyway. He only calls out when the ball is foul.

On a bunt, the bat must not be dropped in fair territory where the ball might roll up against it. This would result in an offensive-interference call.

When hit by a pitch (not seriously) or when receiving a walk, the batter should sprint to first. It is not just a matter of hustle, but it provides a greater amount of time to pick up the signals from the third-base coach and to look over the infield defense.

On a third-strike pitch which is in the dirt or which is dropped by the catcher, the batter should take off for first. However, he might also consider doing so even with first base occupied and less than two out. This is because occasionally the catcher will unnecessarily throw to first anyway. In the process, he may throw the ball away, thus allowing for the advancement of another runner or two.

MAXIMIZING SPEED DOWN THE LINE

Coming out of the batters' box, a low start with a rather pronounced body lean is best. This body lean diminishes quickly as the body arrives at its maximum speed in close to an upright position. The lean continues to exist at an angle of about 25 to 30 degrees from the vertical position.

With an arched neck, the head and eyes should be in line with the base. While the jaw may be relaxed, the runner must not allow his head to sway or flop. This will keep the runner in a straight line so that all of his energy will be expended in a direction perfectly in line with the bag. He will be able to see the play, too.

The length of the stride, which should be close to the runner's height, is determined by the degree of force made by the contact of the runner's rear foot with the ground. To increase speed means either to increase the length of this stride or to increase the repetitions of the present stride. In either case, the runner should be running on the balls of his feet with his toes pointed straight ahead, never out, since such a position would restrict the work of the hips.

The arms come into play when the runner wishes to increase the frequency of his stride. They pump in coordination with the opposite leg. That is, the left arm is pumped forward as the right leg strides forward and vice versa. The arm-pumping is done in a vertical fashion with the hands generally running a route from the hips to the shoulder, but never beyond these limits. To retain proper balance, the runner must never allow his arms to get away from a close-in position to his body. Furthermore, they must not be allowed to swing vertically across the center of the body. All the while, though, the arms are bent at the elbow at an angle of about 90 degrees. Coordination between the arms and legs means that the frequency of leg strides will only increase as the arm pumps increase.

Intentionally removing a helmet while running down the baseline (supposedly to increase speed) not only doesn't help over the short distance involved, but definitely is against the rules in most amateur leagues. The runner would be called out.

Always try to hit the front 4 inches of the bag to make the distance covered from home to first as minimal as possible (Fig. 5-1). Even on a close play, retain your regular stride. Leaping for the bag will actually reduce speed.

Despite what may appear to be an easy-out ground ball, run at full speed all the way to the bag. There are two reasons for this: First, there is always the chance that the throw could be bad or that the first baseman could drop or bobble the ball. Second, even if thrown out, this 90-foot sprint at maximum speed is yet another way of putting pressure on the opposition and will actually be a kind of conditioning drill in preparation for the next trip down the line.

The runner must run "through" the bag so as not to subconsciously slow down as the bag is approached. This simply means trying to visualize the bag as being perhaps 10 feet farther down the line than it actually is. This will assure that the runner is at his maximum speed as the bag is hit.

The first-base coach must never tell the runner to slide into first. Such a decision should come only from the runner himself. Furthermore, it should be attempted only when the first baseman is pulled off the bag by a high throw to the home-plate side of the bag. Anticipating a sweeping, chest-high tag, the runner may **well** be able to avoid such a tag with a slide.

While the 45-foot line must be used on topped balls and bunts, the runner's use of the inside edge of that area will afford him the best chance to reduce the target of the thrower.

Scouts generally consider a fast time to run from home plate to first to be anything under 4.2 seconds for a right-handed batter and under 4 seconds for a left-handed batter.

Figure 5-1   Tagging First Base—As the player runs through the base, his foot makes contact with the nearest four inches of the base.

LISTENING AND WATCHING THE FIRST-BASE COACH

With the ball having been hit to an infielder or outfielder and the runner coming down the line toward first, the first-base coach will react in one of three ways. First, he may respond with an arm signal indicating that the runner should definitely continue to second base. Second, he may give an arm signal indicating that the runner should take a turn and pick up sight of the ball. In this situation, the runner is on his own to determine if he can take another base. He must also be convinced that the game situation is such as to allow for such an advance if it indeed is a "gamble." Third, there may be no signal given at all, indicating that the runner should run through the base at his maximum speed.

There are special situations for which the runner must be his own coach and can't expect help from the first-base coach.

1 As mentioned earlier, on wild infield throws high and to the home plate side of first base, the decision of the runner to slide to avoid a tag must be his own.

2 Following a hard bunt down the first-base line in a sacrifice situation, the runner should slow down or even stop or back up to prevent a possible double play. In this way, more time is given to the advancing runner while the pitcher or first baseman tries to apply a tag on the batter-runner.

3 On a bunt or topped ball fielded near the first-base line, the batter must remember to observe the 45-foot line without the help of the coach.

4 On what appears to be a first-baseman-to-pitcher ground out, the runner should remember that contact with the pitcher in the baseline (before the pitcher has the ball) could result in an obstruction call benefitting the batter-runner. No hard contact is necessary; just a bump will do. Look for that possibility.

AFTER RUNNING THROUGH THE BAG

The stop shouldn't come too quickly since a stumble or fall could easily result. The runner shouldn't allow himself to run too far down the line either. In case of an overthrow, the increased distance to second might make a try to second prohibitive. A slight glance to the right after having passed the bag informs the runner of an errant throw and chance for advancement a split second sooner than hearing it from the first-base coach.

In returning to the bag after having overrun it, the turn back to the infield can be made in either direction. What is important, though, is that no feint be made in the direction of second. Such a move would constitute a turn and make the runner liable to be tagged out. If such a feint is made following a bad throw that gets away from the first baseman, the runner must hurry back to the bag if his decision is not to advance to second. On the other hand, if the runner has not made any such feint, the first baseman may feel otherwise and may start running at him to apply a tag. In no way should the runner jump out of the way to avoid this tag for such a move could be interpreted as a new move to second by the umpire.

ROUNDING THE BAG ON BALLS GOING THROUGH THE INFIELD

In trying to minimize the distance to be run between first and second, the runner must reduce his turning radius as he comes around first. Moving about 3 to 4 feet into foul territory before hitting first will handle this minor problem. For the left-handed hitter, this is easy since he is already in foul territory as he comes out of the batters' box. The right-handed hitter must make a more conscious veering motion. Both types of hitters would do well to try to be at the foul side of the 45-foot line as it is approached 45 feet from the plate. This should produce the desired effect of cutting down the arc formed beyond this turn at first (Fig. 5-2).

Figure 5-2 The Veering Path to First Base—Whether left or right-handed, the batter begins his curved path by hitting a point three feet into foul territory and halfway to first base.

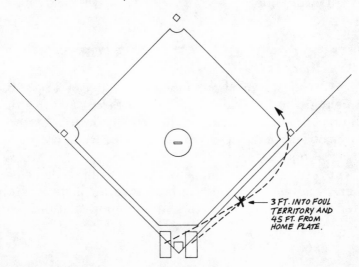

3 FT. INTO FOUL
TERRITORY AND
45 FT. FROM
HOME PLATE.

For a maximum pushoff, the side of the base closest to second should be hit as opposed to the top of the base (Fig. 5-3).

While the runner should not change his stride in any way to hit the bag with any particular leg, there is a slight advantage to hitting it with the inside or left leg. This way, the body makes a sharper turn since the upper body is allowed to dip lower on the turn. This becomes possible since the noncontact leg is on the upside of the turn rather than the downside.

Think of every ball going into the outfield as a possible two bases, making an aggressive turn and being always on the outlook for misplays. Make the outfielders feel pressured. Perhaps they will take their eyes off the ball and let it get through them, or if they do field it properly, they may be forced into making a bad throw.

On the throw back into the infield, continue to watch the ball while returning to the bag after having rounded it. Balls hit to the left half of the outfield are watched over the right shoulder. All others are monitored over the left shoulder.

With a runner on first and a fly ball having just been hit, care must be taken not to pass the runner if he decides to tag and advance after the catch. Of course, if the ball is caught, nothing would be lost. However, if the ball were dropped or fell in for a hit, the batter would be called out for passing a runner.

Be on the lookout for a stunt in which the catcher, or even sometimes the pitcher, sneaks in behind the runner to cover first as the runner is rounding the bag following a hit to right field. The first baseman moves toward the outfield in acting as a decoy. The first-base coach should be able to help the runner if this type of pickoff is attempted.

STRATEGIC CONDITIONS FOR TRYING FOR TWO BASES

Try for two on a hit to a left-handed left fielder or a right-handed right fielder when the ball is between the fielder and the foul line; when no cut man is present or when the throw to the cutoff man goes astray; and on a pop-up to short center when no one bothers to cover second base.

With a runner on second and a ball-four pitch that eludes the catcher, continue to second and try to draw a throw from the catcher which would allow the runner, now at third, to scoot home.

Figure 5-3 Rounding First Base—The base is tagged on that side facing second base to provide for the greatest possible pushoff.

On a fly that drops into short center or short right field, take an aggressive turn at first in hopes of drawing a throw to first. As soon as the outfielder's arm is committed to the throw, break for second.

After hitting a single with a runner on second, take second if no cut is made. Stretching a single into a double is best tried with two outs, almost never with no outs.

With a runner on third trying to score as a result of a ground ball, continue to second if the runner gets caught in a rundown. Be certain that the caught runner is in a position to stay in the rundown long enough to make this aggressive advance possible.

★★

Drills and methods of instruction for Chapter 5 may be found on pages 155–58.

★★

6 ■■■■■■■■■■

Moving from First Base to Second

While many techniques and strategies help the runner on his way to first, it is true, too, that many base runners arrive safely at first without much thought or application of these baserunning tenets. They may have easily arrived through a walk, hit batsman, or a solid hit. For these runners, the arrival at first marks the start of their baserunning thought and strategy. For sure, first base is the launching spot for so much of our baserunning strategy. Because it is the base at which so many pickoffs are attempted, it also becomes the base at which most thought must be given the leadoff: the type, length, stance, and even the return on a pickoff attempt.

How the runner reacts to a ground ball, fly ball, or hit is of immense importance. After all, a lone runner at first might not upset the defense all that much. Allow him to move into scoring position at second, however, and that defense is looking at a problem.

Of course, the baserunning that most people associate with runners at first is the steal. This play is certainly one of the most exciting in baseball and rightly so. If the defense does everything right in trying to stop the steal, it *will* succeed but by only about a tenth of a second. A challenge, then, awaits the aggressive and daring runner. He must find something in his technique that will get him to second base one- or two-tenths of a second sooner than he otherwise would.

The answer may be found in his leadoff, straightaway running, or slide, but the most important determiner of success will be his break. And just how well the runner will be able to distinguish between a pitch and a pickoff will be a direct result of either guesswork or hard study. All too often, guesswork leads to late starts or pickoffs. It is an unsuccessful shortcut to hard work. However, the hard work of studying the pitcher and his pickoff characteristics will pay high dividends. With study, even the average-speed runner will find himself getting super breaks. All he must do is discover the one or two most prominent tip-offs that just about every pitcher exhibits and that differentiates his pitches from his pickoff throws.

Well, it's time to get down into scoring position, so let's get started.

BEFORE STEPPING OFF THE BAG

Be aware of the game situation, including the score, inning, number of outs, and any other men on base. If necessary, get help from the first-base coach. Know the location of the ball, always being on the lookout for a hidden-ball trick. Seeing the pitcher off the mound area (as required by the rules) might be an indication that someone else has the ball.

Don't get into a conversation with the first baseman or even your own first-base coach, so as to remain entirely focused on the game and your purpose on base.

To prevent scraping a hand or jamming a finger on a slide, some runners like to hold grass or dirt in their hands. When sliding they will therefore keep their fists closed. However, the runner must be consistent with this habit, being careful not to do it only when a steal or hit-and-run signal is on.

Look for a signal after every pitch, standing with the left foot on the bag. Continue to watch the third-base coach until he has concluded giving all gestures, both meaningful and otherwise. This makes it more difficult for the opposition to steal any signals.

Following a long foul ball, the runner is wise to pick up the next signal while returning to the bag. This gives the runner more time to assume his next leadoff after retouching the bag.

MOVING OFF THE BAG

To retain a position of balance in leading off, refrain from the use of more than one crossover step; instead, use a technique combining the shuffle step with a slow, sliding motion. Some players like to place the left leg behind the right leg as each slide-step is taken. This is fine since the hips are left in a good position for a quick move back to first if necessary.

The lead begins while the pitcher is on the mound with the ball preparing to toe the rubber to take his sign. While the pitcher is taking that sign, the lead should be completed and held there. This should eliminate the need for assuming a very hurried lead-off. In addition, it will eliminate any advantage that might otherwise be gained by a quick move by the pitcher.

THE TWO-WAY LEAD

Definition and Use

Used with almost every pitch and strategy, this leadoff has as its most striking characteristic an even distribution of weight over both legs. This prepares the runner to move equally well left and right.

The Angle of Leadoff

Basically, there are three angles of leadoff: the front edge, the back edge, and the belly-out. Each type has advantages and disadvantages that must be weighed by the runner in light of the game situation.

In the front-edge leadoff, the heel of the left foot is lined up with the front edge of the bag. The runner will probably receive fewer pickoff throws with this leadoff. This is because the pitcher will see him as part of an optical illusion in which the runner appears closer to the bag than if he were leading off the back edge of the base. In addition, in the case of a grass infield or a somewhat wet or muddy baseline, the runner may be able to get a better footing off a bit of the grassy area.

However, a slight disadvantage appears when the runner tries to return following a pickoff throw, since he now finds himself very close to the first baseman and the tag. This disadvantage can be remedied, though, through a staggering of the feet, which will be discussed in the section "The Stance."

Leading off the back edge of the bag keeps the runner away from the tag of the first baseman. Because of the optical illusion created, however, more pickoff throws can be expected.

The belly-out lead finds the runner still another step back beyond the back edge of the base. It is used when the runner feels the chances of a play on him at second are slim due to the game situation. For instance, the infield may be playing in to cut down a runner from third or the bases may be loaded with the defense again trying to get a play at the plate.

The most important use of this belly-out lead is with the hit-and-run play. Here, the runner is thinking beyond second base and is therefore trying to put himself in a good position to make a sharp turn at second. After all, that's one of the main objectives of the hit-and-run play. Of course, the disadvantage lies in the fact that the runner is actually placing himself a bit farther from second than if he had a more direct-line leadoff. Therefore, it could hurt his chances somewhat if an eventual play is made on him at second. This belly-out lead may also be used when the first baseman is playing off the bag. While it wouldn't be used in a steal situation, it nonetheless is still a two-way lead. The depth of the lead lends itself well to a pickoff attempt so the runner must be aware and cautious.

The Length of the Lead

Many factors will influence the length of the lead. They include the field condition, the runner's reaction time, the importance of the run, and the pitcher's motion and quickness in throwing to first base. With a poor move to first, the pitcher will have a more difficult time holding the runner to a short leadoff.

Some have described the perfect leadoff length as anywhere from 7 to 12 feet or a lead equal to the length of a body and a half. Usually, the lead begins with a crossover step followed by another couple of shuffle steps. What is important, though, in determining the proper length lead is that it be comfortable to the runner and not so great as to find it being converted to a one-way lead. When this happens, it is too long and the runner actually loses some of his aggressiveness. The first-base coach continues to talk to the runner whenever the first baseman plays behind him. A dive back doesn't have to be a requirement of a good lead. Neither should a look back to the bag ever be necessary. This only invites a pickoff attempt.

The Stance (Fig. 6-1)

The back and knees are both bent to provide a lower center of gravity, which in turn provides a greater power thrust when making a move to the left or right. For the greatest possible pushoff, the angle formed between the leg and thigh should be approximately 100 degrees. The body and eyes face the pitcher with the body weight evenly distributed over the balls of the feet.

To keep the body's muscles in a relaxed state, the hands should remain off the knees. The arms and hands (possibly holding dirt in a loose fist) should point forward in a "stick-em-up" fashion or may be left dangling between the legs. The legs should be about shoulder-width apart or just slightly more. Having them too far apart or too close will greatly diminish the thrust of the first step.

In any of the steal or hit-and-run situations, the right foot may be dropped back about 3 inches and actually turned about 45

Figure 6-1 Leadoff Stance—In a two-way leadoff stance, the weight is evenly distributed over the balls of the feet. The hands are off the knees and hanging down inside the two legs.

degrees to better effect that all-important first step toward second. The staggered foot will prevent the runner from running out of a straight line as the crossover step is executed.

The Secondary Lead

The secondary lead amounts to two shuffle steps taken as the pitcher goes to the plate. It is needed to get the body in motion, especially in response to a ground ball. Of course, the secondary lead is used only in non-steal situations.

The key to a good secondary lead lies in the timing. Ideally, the runner wants to be in the process of transferring his weight from his left to his right foot and to be in his second shuffle step at the instant the ball is crossing the plate. If the ball is hit, the runner can simply continue without any staggering or stopping. If the ball isn't hit, he pivots on that right foot as it hits the ground and returns to the bag.

FAKING A BREAK

Bluffing a steal can have many advantages. First, it's disconcerting to the pitcher, especially when he hears his defense yelling out that the runner is going. Second, the shortstop or second baseman will be pulled out of position. Third, the catcher may call for a pitchout out on the next pitch or may be forced to jump up prematurely and, in so doing, possibly take a strike away from his pitcher. Fourth, it may catch the defense sleeping when an actual steal does take place. Fifth, it acts as a practice run for the runner in trying to establish a good jump. Finally, it also lets the runner know who will be covering the bag when the real steal takes place.

The bluff run begins off a strong left leg crossover followed by one more step. To put on the brakes and return to first by facing the infield, the brake must come on the right foot. Therefore, the only other possibility would be a four-step bluff run which would take the runner too far off the bag. Two hard steps, then, represent the ideal fake run.

THE ONE-WAY LEAD

This type of lead helps determine the type of pickoff move employed by the pitcher and helps determine its effectiveness. The runner can then decide just how great a two-way lead he may assume. This type of lead is never used if the steal or hit-and-run play is on. Without such a signal, the one-way lead is taken on the very first pitch.

The one-way lead shouldn't be exaggerated, but great enough to entice the pitcher to throw over to first. The runner will be able to get back safely by keeping the weight on the right foot.

Once the lead is taken, marking the spot with the right foot without taking the eyes off the pitcher helps the runner when he is later determining the length of his two-way lead. If no throw is made, he may wish to try again. The feet should not be staggered in the stance of the one-way lead.

RETURNING TO THE BAG FOLLOWING A PICKOFF ATTEMPT

Despite a runner's speed, that runner must have confidence in his ability to return safely to the base if he intends to utilize that speed.

Although the first-base coach will call out loudly whenever he sees the pitcher beginning a pickoff move, the runner should not rely on the coach to wake him up to this fact. His complete attention should always be on the pitcher, never feeling a reliance on the coach for a cue to return.

Pitchers seldom like to show their best move early. A runner shouldn't allow himself to get lulled into believing that a soft throw indicates the pitcher's best move. The pitcher may be planning to come back with his good move while the same runner is still there.

The Standing Return (Fig. 6-2 and Fig. 6-3)

In a standing return on a soft throw-over, the runner should return to the inside of the bag. This way, he might be able to disrupt the throw by moving into the path of the throw should it be to the second-base side. The runner is entitled to the base path. Further, he is allowed to make contact with the first baseman if the latter enters or reaches into the base path area for a wide throw.

All standing returns begin with a left-foot pivot followed by a right-leg crossover. At this point, runners differ. This is because

Figure 6-2 Standing Return to First (Right-Left-Right)—This return gives
the runner good protection. He can also spot quickly any wild throw.

(Figure 6-2 continued)

Figure 6-3 Standing Return to First (Right-Left)—As the left leg
contacts the outside of the base, the runner swings his body clockwise.
This helps stabilize the stop since the right leg lands near the foul line.

(Figure 6-3 continued)

of the varying distances between the runner and the base. Some runners return in two additional steps, stepping with the left foot and then contacting the bag with the right foot. This amounts to a three-step return. Others return in just one additional step by leaping for the base with their left foot following the crossover step. This, then, is the two-step return.

With the right-left-right return, the runner comes to a halt by stepping into foul territory with a slightly bent left leg. While the runner's face and body might be better protected from a wild pickoff throw this way, it does place him in a poor starting position should the pickoff throw get away.

With the right-left return, the runner contacts the outside of the base with his left foot. He then swings his right leg and side in a clockwise direction so that his right leg lands in foul territory or perhaps on the line itself. This type of return places the runner in a fine starting position should the pickoff throw get away. However, it is also easy for the runner to lose his balance and contact this way. Overall, though, the two-step (right-left) return is preferred mainly because the right foot provides a firm foundation in taking off for second. In addition, the direction of the body allows for a quick sighting of the throw.

The Diving Return (Fig. 6-4)

The technique for the dive-return begins with a forceful left-foot pivot followed by a strong crossover with the right leg. Care should be taken so as not to begin with a jab action of the left foot, which represents a waste of time. In addition, the crossover of the right leg must be hard enough to prevent the runner's body from veering back toward the infield and inside of the bag.

Now, with a strong thrust produced by the low lean of the body and bent right leg, the runner dives toward the outside corner of the bag. The right hand reaches for the corner of the base while the left hand remains out of the way in the direction of right field. The fully extended body and outstretched hands should make contact with the ground just about simultaneously. The knees should not hit the ground first. Failing to get the left hand out from under the body could cause finger injuries and could also produce a bouncy landing.

Figure 6-4 Diving Return—The dive begins with a forceful crossover followed by a body extension. It results with the right hand on the outside corner of the base and the left hand clear of the body.

(Figure 6-4 continued)

(Figure 6-4 continued)

THE SACRIFICE BUNT

In this situation, the runner breaks for second only after he is sure that contact has been made and that the bunt has not been popped up. Therefore, he should try to time the landing of the second shuffle step of his secondary lead with this anticipated result. The mistake is made when the runner tries to time this step with bat contact only.

If the ball is handled down the third-base line and the runner sees no one covering third, he should consider taking third even though this may not have been the original intention of the play. He should be relatively sure, though, of making it safely to third. This is especially true with two outs, since staying at second would still leave him in scoring position.

FLY BALLS

Whenever a line drive is determined to be coming off the bat of the batter, the runner must freeze in his tracks as he concludes his secondary lead, assuming less than two outs. He continues only when the ball is seen passing beyond the infielders. While in the frozen position, the runner must prepare to return quickly in case the ball is caught by shifting most of the weight to the lead foot.

On any foul fly ball, the runner returns to the bag and tags for a possible advancement. By returning for a tag up, there is nothing to lose and everything to gain. If the fly ball is deep enough, an advancement may be possible after the catch, especially with a weak-armed or lackadaisical outfielder.

On catchable fly balls hit into the deep-gap areas as well as into deep center and right fields, advancing after a tag up is a reasonable gamble with less than two outs. This is especially true when the outfielder's arm is the least bit suspect. There must be relative certainty, though, that the ball will be caught. There must be certainty, too, that the game situation could tolerate such an aggressive gamble at that point.

With both routine and shallow flies that stand some chance of dropping in, the runner should move up the line without tagging up. How far up the line he moves depends upon the location of the ball as well as the strength of the outfielder's arm. If the ball is caught, he continues to watch the throw-in while returning just in case the throw goes astray.

FOLLOWING A GROUND BALL

With Two Outs   If the play is being made at first, the runner should round second base and pick up sight of the ball in case the batter is safe for any reason. If the play instead is made at second, he should execute a pop-up slide since the ball could be dropped. Never go in standing.

With Less than Two Outs   Again, if the play is to first, he should round the bag and pick up sight of the ball. If the play is to second, the runner must break up any possible double play by taking out the pivot man. Both the roll slide and the bent-leg slide used to upset the pivot man have been described in the chapter on sliding. If the pivot man is the second baseman, he most likely will come across the bag to turn the double play. Therefore, the slide should be to the inside of the bag. On the other hand, when the pivot man is the shortstop, he will usually come across to the right-field side of the bag. If this is the case, the slide should be to the outside of the bag.

The runner is not allowed to leave the baseline totally to get at the infielder. He must remain close enough to make some contact with the bag as well as the pivot man. There will always be a certain amount of guessing as to just which side the pivot man will move as he approaches the bag. It is helpful to watch the second baseman's style of turning double plays during his infield practice. The runner can then use this stored knowledge in deciding just where to go down in his takeout slide.

Consider a ground ball to second with less than two outs. The second baseman may try to tag the runner in the base path and then throw to first to complete a double play. The runner shouldn't hand the defense such an easy double play without a good fight. True, the defense has the upper hand here, but the runner has some options, too. He should back up toward first to avoid a tag. If he eventually is tagged, he may have been successful in delaying the play long enough to allow the batter to reach first safely. If the second baseman instead decides to throw to first in lieu of tagging the runner, the latter may be able to beat the return throw to second by the first baseman. Remember that this becomes a tag play now that the force has been removed, and a hook slide could find the runner safe.

Another situation finds a ground ball hit behind the runner with less than two outs. The runner is unaware of whether an infielder is fielding the ball or whether it has gone through for a hit. If the ball is fielded, the infielder will probably want to go to second for a force, if not a double play. Therefore, the runner should run upright in hopes of either being hit by the throw or helping obscure the vision of the shortstop as the throw approaches.

If the runner knows the ball will be fielded by the second baseman, he should veer more toward the right-field side of the bag. That would likely represent the line the throw would take. The position that the shortstop takes to receive the throw should also be a tip-off. When the runner sees no one covering the bag, he should pick up sight of the third-base coach for instructions since the ball probably got through the infield for a hit. The give-and-take of such signals will be discussed in the next sections.

THOUGHTS OF GOING TO THIRD

On a ball hit behind the runner, help must be received from the third-base coach. With about a third of the way still to go toward second, the runner picks up sight of the coach. The coach's arm signals will be the same as those used with a runner coming into third. Waving his arms in a circular motion indicates that he wants the runner to continue to third. Both arms held overhead indicates that the runner should round the bag and pick up sight of the ball, but should not attempt to advance beyond that point unless some miscue arises. One arm overhead and the other pointing at the bag differs only in that the runner should stop on the bag without rounding it. This is because it probably appears to the coach that a throw is about to be made to second by the outfielder handling the ball. A pop-up slide is best used here to prevent the runner from overrunning the base.

The coach will also be giving verbal directions. However, even when the coach has signaled the runner to advance to third, he may occasionally see reason to change his mind. For that reason, it's important that the runner pick up sight of the coach a second time just after having rounded second.

The runner is on his own whenever the ball is hit in front of him. Just how daring he should be in this situation depends on a number of factors, most important of which are the number of outs, the importance of his run, and the batting order of the hitters to follow. Chances shouldn't be taken with two outs unless the bottom of the batting order is coming up. That is why it's so important to know the makeup of the order when on base. Again, such decisions will be made by the coach when the ball is hit behind the runner. Only when the hit ball is in plain view of the runner will this decision rest with him.

Statistically, the best time to take chances is with one out. It is preferable not to begin the next inning with the ninth man in the batting order hitting, especially if he's the pitcher. When a base hit is hit directly at an outfielder, the odds are with the outfielder in throwing the runner out at third. However, the odds turn quickly in favor of the runner if the outfielder must move more than a couple of steps to his left or right.

THE HIT-AND-RUN

This play finds the runner breaking for second with the pitch. The batter's job is not only to make contact, but to try to send the ball to the right side of the diamond. This way, both objectives of the play will have been met. First, the double-play possibility will be removed, and second, the runner has an excellent chance of advancing to third. Because the runner need not be fast, it is important for the batter to protect him. Even if the pitch isn't just where he would like it, he must try to get at least a piece of the ball.

In determining the length of leadoff for the hit-and-run, bear in mind that the best defense against this play is the pitchout. Chances are that a pitchout would indeed be called if the defense felt the play coming. On the one hand, then, the leadoff should be shortened slightly to conceal the play. This way, the chances of a pitchout would be minimal. On the other hand, a longer leadoff gives the runner a better start and would also likely cause the second baseman to play a step or two closer to second. This would open even more of the right side of the infield. And, of course, that is just where the hitter is trying to put the ball. Keep both these advantages and disadvantages in mind in assuming the lead.

Regardless of the length of lead, it should be of the belly-out type, a step behind the back side of the bag. If the batter succeeds in hitting the ball through the right side, this lead will facilitate the rounding of second on the way to third.

As the pitcher commits himself to the pitch, the runner breaks, trying to time a look in toward the plate to coincide with the instant the ball will be hit. This will occur on about the fourth step and will allow time for the runner to pick up sight of the ball. This is especially important if the ball is hit in the air.

If the ball is hit in front of the runner, he decides for himself whether or not to proceed to third. If the ball is hit behind him, he looks to the third-base coach as discussed earlier. However, before doing so, he should first take a quick peek over his right shoulder to determine whether the ball has gone through in case there was any doubt. This will help, too, in preventing the runner from being decoyed by the shortstop into thinking that the ball was handled by the second baseman.

If the pitch is fouled away, the runner should look to the coach on his way back to first to learn whether the play is still on. This will save him time to assume his next leadoff.

THE MENTAL ASPECTS OF STEALING

The mental prerequisites to stealing are desire and confidence. The runner should realize that the lower the level of ball, the poorer will be the skills of the pitcher in holding him on base and the poorer will be the quickness, strength, and accuracy of the catcher's arm. Helping, too, will be the runner's confidence in his own speed. Often, it will be close to or even equal to that of his professional counterpart. Acquiring confidence is the most challenging part of the battle. The player must constantly assure himself of his knowledge of the pitcher and his moves, his own reflexes and speed, his ability to get a good lead and jump, and his mastery of the techniques of sliding.

The runner must put any fear of failure completely out of his mind. If he ever does get thrown out, he won't get "down." In fact, he won't even be afraid of being thrown out or picked off, although he will naturally try always to avoid these mishaps. When these things happen, he will just work all the harder for his next attempt. He will continue to tell himself that his ability to run the bases far surpasses the abilities of the pitcher and catcher to keep him planted.

THE GENERALITIES OF STUDYING THE PITCHER

Studying the pitcher's moves is best accomplished from the outfield end of the first-base dugout. It provides the best viewing angle.

The first runner on base should attempt to draw a throw so that the entire team can get an early look at his move. A one-way lead is used for this purpose. In addition, the runner may also wish to fake a break to determine early which infielder will go to the bag and just how quickly the middle infielders will open the infield for a hit-and-run-play possibility.

Besides studying the pitcher, a base runner's decision to steal or not (if he is on his own) is influenced by the game situation. This includes the score, the number of outs, the ability of the batter, the strength of the catcher's arm, and the importance of his run.

With pitchers whose delivery to the plate is quick, but whose move to first is mediocre at best, the runner would be wise to take a longer leadoff. On the other hand, with pitchers having good moves, but whose kicks and deliveries to the plate are slow, the confident base runner should have a field day with even an average leadoff.

Before checking various body parts characterizing whether a pitcher will throw to home or to first, keep this is mind: Almost every pitcher, including the lefties, is committed in his own mind as to what he intends to do following his stop at the end of the stretch. This is great news for base runners who sometimes think that pitchers (especially lefties), after deciding to throw home with a pitch, will change their minds and go to first the instant the runner takes off.

However, most lefty pitchers say that this is very difficult for them to do and, consequently, they will follow through with their original plans. If a plan was to throw home, that is exactly where the ball will go even if a runner is seen beginning a break for second.

STUDYING THE RIGHT-HANDED PITCHER

The right-handers have five positions from which to throw to first although they usually tend to stick to a favored two or three. The five positions are: (1) while looking in for the sign, (2) while going up, (3) at the very top, (4) while coming down, and (5) after coming set. While the fifth position presents the least surprise to the runner, it is still the most popular. Furthermore, it is not until after the pitcher has had the opportunity to throw over from this fifth position that the runner can break for second. Fortunately for the runner, every right-handed pitcher, when studied carefully, will display one or more telltale characteristics that will inform the runner of his intentions. Those characteristics will be described in the following paragraphs.

The Front and Rear Heels (Fig. 6-5)

With the pitcher throwing to the plate, his front (left) heel must clear the ground as he begins his kick. Although his entire front foot will lift, the action is almost always inaugurated by the heel as opposed to the whole foot, which lifts at the same time. While this action is going on, the back (right) foot remains flat against the rubber. However, on the pickoff attempt at first, it will be the back heel that lifts as the pitcher begins his jump or begins his step back off the rubber. Of course, on the jump to first, the front foot will also move and lift, but always following the movement of the back heel and foot. Therefore, the runner knows that if the first movement is by that of the front heel, the pitcher will throw home. If the pitcher's first movement is by that of the rear heel, the pitcher

Figure 6-5   Front and Rear Heels—On a pickoff attempt, the right heel lifts first, while the left heel lifts first on a pitch to the plate.

(Figure 6-5 continued)

is coming to first. The only disadvantage of using this characteristic is that the runner must train his eyes to focus on two parts of the pitcher's body simultaneously. He must watch both the front and back heels, and then react accordingly.

The Head and Cap (Fig. 6-6)

To get a better view of the runner, some pitchers will turn the head slightly toward first and at the same time dip the head and cap downward. On a pickoff, the head and cap will often remain in that position as the pitcher pivots to throw. On a pitch, though, the pitcher will first raise his head and cap to its normal position before pitching. To avoid giving away their intentions, the better pitchers will often bob their heads once or twice before making their intended move. The less experienced pitchers, however, will leave out the bob, thus providing the runner with a telltale characteristic.

Figure 6-6   The Head and Cap—With the head and cap dipped downward for a better look at the runner, some pitchers will begin their pickoff attempts from this position. To pitch, they will lift the head without any bobbing.

(Figure 6-6 continued)

The Shoulder (Fig. 6-7)

Some pitchers, to get a better view of the runner, will open up their front shoulder to first. Of course, in throwing to first, that shoulder will open even more. However, even though this turned shoulder does provide a better view, it carries the disadvantage of having to be closed again when the pitcher decides to throw home. This takes some added time, but more important, it provides the runner with an added characteristic to cue on. The instant the runner sees that open shoulder begin to close, he should feel confident in breaking. A throw to first after the pitcher has begun closing and kicking would constitute a balk.

Figure 6-7   The Shoulder—An exaggerated open left shoulder provides an excellent cue for the break for second. The shoulder must close a great deal for the pitch home.

(Figure 6-7 continued)

The Body Lean (Fig. 6-8)

A few pitchers come set with their feet next to each other rather than in a more balanced postion. As a consequence, this type of pitcher will often place most of his weight on his back leg, demonstrate practically no leg lift, and be in a hurry to get rid of the ball because of his awareness of the runner. His whole body, then, begins to tilt or lean forward toward the plate before he actually begins to deliver the ball. When this pitcher does wish to throw over, he will assume a more balanced set position. However, when the runner does detect the shoulder and body beginning to lean, he can use it as his cue to break.

Figure 6-8   The Body Lean—Pitchers who come set with their legs together often give away their intention to throw home by leaning toward home just as they are about to begin their kick. Their pickoffs are from a more upright position.

(Figure 6-8 continued)

The Left Knee (Fig. 6-9)

In throwing home, the tendency of the pitcher is to bend back the left knee as the kick is begun. However, in throwing to first, there is no bending in this knee. Instead, the runner sees an outward rotation toward first as the pitcher begins his jump in that direction.

The Front Elbow (Fig. 6-9)

Just like the left knee, the front elbow generally follows a parallel flight pattern. When the pitcher throws home, the front elbow begins to curl inward just as the shoulder and front knee do. Besides curling inward, it will also move upward, thus exposing the underarm area. When throwing to first, the pitcher's elbow is pushed outward in the direction of first. In other words, elbow in and/or up, he is going home; elbow out, he is coming to first.

Figure 6-9   The Left Knee and Elbow—Throwing home, the pitcher's elbow and knee both curl toward the front of the pitcher's body and away from the runner. In the pickoff, both the elbow and knee become more and more exposed as they turn outward.

(Figure 6-9 continued)

The High Kicker (Fig. 6-10)

While the batter who has to face the high kicker may not have any particular advantage, the runner does. Although the pitcher may be able to get a little more velocity on the ball, he will also have to give up some precious tenths of seconds. What the pitcher gives up in delivery time actually becomes extra time handed to the runner.

Figure 6-10   The High Kicker—This is the ideal pitcher to study due to the excessive time he takes to deliver the ball to the plate.

The Head Direction (Fig. 6-11)

Another characteristic to watch for in some pitchers is the look toward third as he is coming set. The pitcher tries to make the runner believe that he is being careless in not keeping an eye on him. In reality, the pitcher is readying himself for a throw to the base. Yet, when intent on throwing home, he will usually continue to watch the runner out of the side of his eye rather than looking

Figure 6-11   The Head Direction—Watch for the right-handed pitcher who throws to first despite a head direction directly toward third before the throw. When throwing home, the eyes are first fixed on the runner.

(Figure 6-11 continued)

directly to third. Other pitchers have a signal system worked out with the third baseman who will let the pitcher know when a throw to first is in order. With such a system, the pitcher never looks over to the runner since there is no need. However, while appearing to be an advantage, this characteristic also acts to tip off the opposition that such a system is being employed.

STUDYING THE LEFT-HANDED PITCHER

Runners often feel more intimidated when trying to steal against a left-handed pitcher. Perhaps it is because the pitcher is facing him. Perhaps, too, it may be simply because runners don't get a chance to see as many lefties as righties. However, the lefties will often give away their moves in as many different ways as the righties. It just takes a little study of the telltale characteristics.

The Head Direction (Fig. 6-12)

Most pitchers like to do one of two things as they begin their kicks. One group will watch the runner as long as possible before throwing home. When throwing to first, they will look home as the kick is started. Another group will do just the opposite. This group will keep their eyes on the plate when throwing there and will watch the runner as the kick is made preceding the throw to first. Determining that a pitcher is consistent in using one of these two methods will help the base runner immensely.

   Of course, it's assumed that such a pitcher is not breaking the plane of the rubber as the initial movement of the kick is made. Otherwise this would greatly diminish whatever deception he might have held over the runner originally. Pitchers that fall into either of these two categories can still create some confusion for the runner with a slight delay at the top of the kick. The pitchers with the really fine moves, though, won't let themselves fall into either of these categories. Instead, they will mix the placement of their eyes as they begin their kick. With such pitchers, the runner must look for other telltale characteristics.

Figure 6-12   The Head Direction—Some left-handed pitchers *always* begin by looking in the opposite direction of the throw. While in the kick, the look is to home but the throw is to first. Otherwise, the pitcher looks to first but throws home.

(Figure 6-12 continued)

(Figure 6-12 continued)

The Upraised Chin and Arched Chest and Back (Fig. 6-13)

As the pitcher kicks just prior to a pickoff attempt, he will often try to pause to deceive the runner. But, in so doing he often will give away his intentions by throwing his chest out in an arched manner with the shoulders pulled back. He will also often tilt the left shoulder farther back than the right. This doesn't happen when the pitcher throws home. Delivering to the plate, his chest will be fully in view and almost perfectly erect so as to produce as much push off the rubber as possible. In addition, nothing of note takes place with the pitcher's chin, but with the arched position in throwing to first, the chin will move up and often back, too. This is a very apparent characteristic that can be easily seen by the runner.

The arching of the back is slightly more difficult to detect although it is very easily spotted by the third-base coach. To produce a truly great move, a pitcher must not only pause slightly at the top of his kick, but must also keep his upper body erect and his chin down. Because few pitchers work hard enough at these points, the runner will often be able quickly to determine the pitcher's intentions by watching for these characteristics.

Figure 6-13 The Upraised Chin and Arched Chest and Back—Note the level head and chin and the squared upper body on the pitch home. The pickoff move is characterized by an uneven chest, head, chin and back.

(Figure 6-13 continued)

(Figure 6-13 continued)

The Height of the Leg Kick (Fig. 6-14)

In throwing to the plate, the pitcher will usually try to get a little more velocity through a harder push off the rubber. He accomplishes this through the help of a higher leg kick. When throwing to first, the pitcher will not kick as high because of his concern for good balance on his left leg as he quickly pivots the left foot for the throw. When this difference in the height of the kick is substantial, it can be an easy characteristic for the runner to spot as he tries to ascertain the pitcher's intentions.

Figure 6-14 The Height of the Leg Kick—Some pitchers exhibit a distinct difference in the height of their leg kicks depending upon their intentions. The high leg kick is usually associated with the pitch home while the low kick tips-off the oncoming pickoff attempt.

(Figure 6-14 continued)

Body Lean (Fig. 6-15)

Some pitchers, in their haste to throw home, get into the habit of assuming a momentary "Leaning Tower of Pisa" appearance as they are about to kick and deliver. Because this premature weight shift moves the pitcher's body toward the plate, it prohibits the pitcher from throwing to first. Such a change in the direction of the right shoulder would result in a balk call. Therefore, as soon as the runner notes this lean, he should make his break. A few pitchers will similarly demonstrate a lean not to the plate but to first while beginning the kick at the same time. With the lean to first, the runner, of course, should return quickly to first.

Figure 6-15 Body Lean—When some lefties come set with both feet together, they will often give away their intention to pitch home with a premature lean in that direction.

Breaking the Plane of the Rubber (Fig. 6-16)

Pitching rules stipulate that the pitcher must throw home whenever any part of his right foot, knee, or leg breaks the imaginary front plane of the rubber. While such a break may provide the pitcher with a little something extra, it also serves as a tip-off for prospective base stealers. The smart left-hander will not allow his kick to break the plane as his leg is being raised. Instead, the runner will be kept guessing. The smart pitcher will raise his leg vertically. Otherwise, the runner will be off and running as soon as such a break is detected.

Figure 6-16 Breaking the Plane of the Rubber—The sight of a right knee or leg breaking the plane of the rubber should act as a green light for the runner intent on stealing.

(Figure 6-16 continued)

The Right Foot and Knee (Fig. 6-17)

Some pitchers give away their intentions through the actions of their lead foot as their kick is started. Watch for the pitcher who will turn up his toes toward his body, thus showing the sole of his right shoe to the runner. Most pitchers who do this will go home with the ball. When they wish to go to first, their toes will point down rather than up, and the sole will not be visible. A few pitchers do just the opposite, though. What is important to the runner is that the pitcher demonstrate these two distinct and opposite foot movements consistently. If this consistency is lacking or if the characteristic is lacking entirely, this tip-off possibility must be abandoned.

In like manner, some pitchers have a tendency to turn in the right foot or knee (or both) toward second even though they may not break the plane of the rubber. From such a move, these pitchers will usually go home with the ball, feeling that such a movement will add some "pop" to their pitches. When throwing to first, the foot or knee (or both) will move straight up without any turn toward second. Sometimes, it is just the other way around; but again, the runner must be relatively assured of consistency or look for a different tip-off characteristic.

Figure 6-17 The Right Foot and Knee—Some pitchers consistently expose the instep of their right foot on a pickoff attempt. On the pitch home, the sole of that foot is exposed. Some pitchers do it the very opposite.

(Figure 6-17 continued)

The Leg Gap (Fig. 6-18)

In throwing to first, the pitcher will often kick more in the direction of the first-base dugout than directly toward the bag. In this way, he feels that he can better conceal his intentions. It will appear as if he is moving in the direction of the plate as he merely uses the maximum allowable angle in the placement of his right foot. However, there is a drawback to this method that should interest the runner. When the pitcher kicks to throw to first, the inner side of his right thigh becomes immediately visible to the runner. On a pitch to the plate, the pitcher's right knee will conceal the inner thigh since the leg will move straight up rather than out toward the plate. If this proves to be a consistent pattern, the runner should respond accordingly. If he sees only knee on the kick, he goes. If he sees the inner side of the thigh, he anticipates a throw to the bag.

The Consistent Looker

Occasionally, a pitcher will be observed who will look directly at the runner on every kick whether throwing home or to first. Eventually, he will turn his head toward home to pick up his target if his intention is to throw home. However, when throwing to first, he will try to deceive the runner into thinking he is going home by turning his head from the runner to a downward tilt position. From there, he will turn his head back toward the runner again as the throw is made there. The key is the tilt. If the turn of the head from the runner is made directly to the plate, the pitcher is going home with the ball. However, if the head turn is more of a downward tilt, the runner can anticipate the pickoff throw. Again, the consistency of this characteristic must be present if it is to be used to the runner's advantage.

The Short Leadoff-Sleeper Ploy

While not a pitching characteristic, this is a stunt that a runner can use against a left-handed pitcher, especially one with a good move. Instead of taking his usual, aggressive leadoff, the runner instead takes not even an average leadoff, but a short one. It should be a leadoff conveying the message that this runner is not

Figure 6-18   The Leg Gap—Left-handed pitchers sometimes give away their pickoff intentions by exposing the inner left thigh on their kick. On their pitch home, this area is not visible to the runner as the kick is made.

(Figure 6-18 continued)

interested in stealing. Consequently, he is not about to get picked off by assuming a big leadoff. This is done for at least the first two pitches. As a result, the pitcher decides early that throwing to first would be a waste of time. After all, the runner isn't going anywhere with that kind of leadoff, so the pitcher will concentrate instead on the batter.

Assuming that this isn't one of those pitchers who almost stop at the height of their kicks, the runner can break as soon as the pitcher makes any kind of movement. He doesn't look for any characteristic whatsoever. Instead, he is gambling that the pitcher's movement is one toward the plate. As a result, the runner will probably find himself farther down the baseline as the ball is released than if the normal, aggressive two-way lead were taken. Of course, the runner is gambling that the pitcher won't throw over, but the odds in this case should be in his favor. He can also allow himself the added advantage of assuming a reversed, one-way leadoff from his shortened-up position.

The Long Leadoff-Sleeper Ploy

This is a stunt that begins with the runner assuming his usual, aggressive leadoff. However, for the first two or three pitches, his first move is back toward the bag as the pitcher begins his kick. It really amounts to an exaggerated one-way leadoff, for not only is the runner's weight on his right foot, but the runner also makes an exaggerated move back toward the bag. He acts intimidated by the fact that the pitcher is left-handed. The idea is to make the pitcher feel that he has the runner scared and confused and certainly not a steal threat. With this impression, the pitcher is not about to throw over. Then, on about the third or fourth pitch, the runner instead breaks toward second rather than back to first. It still represents a gamble, of course, but one not nearly as risky. Chances are slim that a pickoff would be attempted here when, on every previous pitch, the runner has jumped back to the base.

THE LOGISTICS OF THE STEAL

This is it! The steal sign has been flashed. The coach has determined that the steal is a sound, strategic play in this situation and well worth the risk. The runner has an idea of both the pitcher's delivery move as well as his pickoff move. He has mentally painted a picture of the exact moment when he will make his break. He has assumed his leadoff. In his stance, he is bent at the waist and knees, with his weight over the balls of his feet. His legs are comfortably spread and his arms are hanging down and off his knees. Care is taken not to lean either forward or toward second. A pickoff throw takes the pitcher approximately one second to complete. With the runner being able to cover 90 feet in about 4 seconds, this breaks down to 11¼ feet per second. Therefore, it is not unreasonable for a runner with quick reflexes to assume a leadoff of about 11 feet. Even without a super break, this would leave the runner with about seven-eighths of the distance still to be covered in 3½ seconds. But the question is, "Will the ball beat him there?"

Well, it takes the average pitcher about one full second to release the ball out of the set position. With that second gone by, the runner will now find himself at least three-eighths of the way to second. The ball will now be coming out of the pitcher's hand. Another half second will pass before a pitcher's 74-mph fast ball will travel the remaining 54 feet to the plate. His hand will be approximately 6 ½ feet in front of the rubber at the point of release. The distance that the ball must travel, then, is reduced from 60 ½ feet to about 54 feet.

A pitcher will usually achieve a 74-mph fast ball during his high school years. If his speed is less than 74 mph, slightly more than a half second will be needed for the ball to pass from the pitcher's hand to the catcher's mitt. The required time will be even longer with an off-speed pitch. Most curve balls, for example, are thrown at a speed about 10 mph less than the pitcher's fast ball. This means that the pitcher who throws the 74-mph fast ball (requiring 0.5 seconds to reach the catcher's mitt) will deliver his curve ball at about 64 mph. At this speed, the time needed for the ball to reach the catcher equals 0.58 seconds, almost a tenth of a second longer for this off-speed pitch. Obviously, the required time for the pitch to reach the catcher will be proportionately greater for pitchers unable to throw a 74-mph fast ball.

The runner is now half of the way to second. The time needed for the catcher to pivot, cock his arm, and throw is close to another full second while the throw, catch, and tag will take still another second. Whatever the breakdown between the catcher's handling of the ball and the throw itself, the total time involved for the catcher's involvement in the play totals about 2 seconds. Of course, it should be noted that this scenario pits a fast runner against both a fast pitcher and a good-throwing catcher. Even so, if the pitcher, catcher, and infielder have done everything perfectly, the runner will probably be out on a bang-bang play with the out-safe margin being approximately one-tenth of a second. And this is the way it should be!

The steal should be considered a risk. In fact, the one-tenth-second margin will be even greater with runners who take shorter leadoffs, get poorer jumps, or simply cannot cover 90 feet in 4 seconds. However, the odds can quickly shift in favor of the base runner who can get the good leadoff, can get the good jump, and can cover 90 feet in 4 seconds.

And let's not forget the defense! They don't always perform their functions with perfection. The pitcher may fail to check the leadoff of the runner, may be slow with his release, may throw an off-speed pitch, may throw a pitch that is difficult to handle, or may make a completely wild pitch. The catcher may drop the ball, juggle it, catch it off balance, be slow in releasing it, make a less than hard throw to second, throw it off the mark making it difficult to handle, or make a completely wild throw out of the reach of the infielder. The infielder may be slow in getting to the bag, may drop or juggle the ball, may miss the tag, or may have the ball kicked out of his mitt through the work of the runner's slide. Therefore, whether the runner is fast or average, there are just so many ways that he can overcome that small margin built into the game to favor the defense on the steal.

A breakdown of the time involved in the act of stealing will often resemble this sequence.

Figure 6-19 Timeline of a Steal—Notice that the runner is usually one-third of the distance to second by the time that the pitcher releases the ball.

THE BREAK TO SECOND (Fig. 6-20)

The most-advocated start to second begins with a quick right-foot pivot followed by a strong left-leg crossover. This movement of the left leg can be facilitated by dropping the right leg back an inch or two in the stance. This will also keep the runner from running outside a direct line to second. Otherwise, the crossover will actually draw the runner to the infield side of the baseline because his right leg and side will be in the way. The crossover maneuver will produce a stronger and longer step covering more ground on this important first step than stepping first with the right foot. Simulating a left-handed uppercut will also help to square the runner's body to second more quickly and should also help to accelerate that step even more.

Then, with head down and body low and arms driving, the takeoff continues with the second, third, and fourth steps. It is crucial that on the first step, the shoulders (especially the right)

Figure 6-20   The Break to Second—This most conventional and most used break begins from a slightly staggered two-way leadoff. It follows with a strong pivot and left leg crossover.

(Figure 6-19 continued)

(Figure 6-20 continued)

(Figure 6-20 continued)

remain thrust forward, producing considerable body lean in the upper body. The strong push off the bent right leg should not be allowed to place the runner in an upright position after just a step or two. In fact, during the first few strides out of the blocks, championship sprinters find themselves in a 40- to 45-degree forward body lean, that angle being formed between the ground and a line running through the toes of the back foot, the knee cap, the thigh, trunk, and head. Further, the super base runners continue to maintain that kind of lean all the way to the next base, actually allowing the force of gravity to work in their favor. This is because such a lean forces the legs to work harder to keep the body from falling over completely.

It has been shown that championship caliber sprinters don't reach their maximum velocity until they have run about 165 feet, which is more than 1 ½ baselines. This tells us that the good base runner should find himself accelerating all the way up to the point of his slide. Then, if the runner uses a head-first slide, that forward body lean and continuing acceleration will lose almost no momentum as the player lowers his upper body for the slide. A feet-first slide will lose slightly more since the forward lean must first become converted to a backward lean to allow the feet to come into the base ahead of the upper body.

Unless the take sign is on, the runner should have a look in to the plate over his left shoulder at the time the ball is arriving at the plate. Such a look is easiest when the right leg is hitting the ground. This would mean an even-numbered step. The second step is definitely too early since the ball would still be on its way to the plate. The sixth would be too late. The fourth, then, becomes the ideal step at which to have the look in toward the plate. Despite good intentions and proper mechanics, however, a runner might still fail to get a good jump. Poor field conditions or a confusing move by the pitcher might be the reason. When this occurs, the runner should use discretion and return to the bag rather than being thrown out needlessly. Any type of hesitation or staggering will surely cost the runner those precious tenths of seconds needed to arrive at second safely.

A second method of making the initial break for second has recently been espoused and has experienced a growing following (Fig. 6-21). Its techniques, for the most part, directly contradict those of the more-popular method described in the last para-

Figure 6-21 Alternate Break for Second—Note the more upright stance. The break begins with a pushoff the left leg and immediately places the runner in the proper arm/leg sync.

graph. Proponents criticize the crossover method by claiming that the runner is in too low a position in the stance, a stance that places the arms low and legs more than shoulder-width apart. From this position, it is claimed that the runner must first waste a lot of motion before the body can take a step in a normal stride. After all, this won't take place until about the fourth step. Furthermore, as the crossover is made, the quick turn of the right side of the body also has a twisting effect upon the shoulders. The result finds the body being thrown slightly toward right field. The runner must then work to get his body back on line during the next couple of steps. Most important, though, is the criticism that the crossover method finds the runner's left arm and leg moving forward simultaneously on the first step. No runner can continue this same-arm, same-leg technique very long. It is simply contradictory to proper running style. In adjusting to the left-leg, right-arm and right-leg, left-arm proper technique, the runner must again waste time. To remedy these drawbacks, the runner makes some changes in this relatively new type of break.

Using a very slight, but comfortable, squat, the runner assumes a stance that places his arms close to his body and up toward his waist. The feet are spread no more than shoulder-width apart. The big difference, however, lies in the first step. Instead of driving off the right leg with the help of a left-leg crossover, the first step begins with a *push* off the left leg. It might seem that this amounts to the first step's being taken by the right foot, but such a statement would be misleading. It was once described by an advocate as similar to "leaping off the side of a curb." Therefore, it is, indeed, more of a pushoff of the left leg. It really is not a leap because the body does not fly into the air nor does the right leg reach out far toward second.

To encourage acceleration, the knee of the right leg must come down into a position approximately below the right shoulder. What is especially important is that this type of start immediately places the runner into proper running position since the first movement couples the left-arm drive with the right-leg step. Yet, critics of this method point to both the longer first step of the crossover method and the acceleration given that first step by the left-cross action of the left arm. Only by experimentation with both methods and stopwatch timings will a runner be able to determine just which method works best for him.

A third type of break to second is the one employed in the delayed steal. It is best utilized when the catcher lazily receives pitches and in like manner returns them to the pitcher. It also works when the middle infielders fail to pay the runner proper attention, or when they have the habit of turning their backs to the infield once the pitch has been received. Instead of taking the usual two shuffle steps in the secondary lead, the runner takes three shuffle steps, and then goes into a sprint to second. Often the defense will be taken by surprise.

The fourth and final type of break is the one resulting from the walking lead. It was popularized by Maury Wills, who often used it with great success against less-experienced pitchers. As the pitcher begins to take his set position, the runner casually walks off first and does not assume any kind of stance. Instead, he breaks for second without coming to a stop as the pitcher makes his move to throw home. Because the body is already facing second and slowly moving in that direction, a good jump is assured. It can also be used following a pitcher's pickoff attempt if it appears that he then wants to quick-pitch before the runner can set up in a regular leadoff stance.

However, pitchers who are more experienced will seldom allow a runner to take a lead without making him come to a stop. It certainly represents a risk to the runner since he finds himself in a very poor position from which to return on a pickoff attempt.

EVADING THE RUNDOWN

While it is not an envied position, the rundown is a play that runners occasionally get caught in on a pickoff attempt or through some other circumstance. Good defense should win out and usually in just one throw. Therefore, the runner must look for some help in this situation. It might come in the form of a poorly timed throw, a wild throw, a throw that hits the runner, a dropped throw, or an obstruction call made against a defensive player. The more throws that a runner can force the defense to make, the better will be his chance of forcing some form of error.

However, with each reversal in the base path, the runner loses more and more energy. In being chased, he should keep an eye over his shoulder to see just when a throw is being made. If it appears that the defensive player may be holding the ball too long, a break for the next base is a good idea. As the runner begins his break for the base, he should turn completely toward that base and watch the eyes of the defensive player who will be receiving the ball. He tries to determine the path that the throw will take and tries to remain in that path. His hope is either to get hit with the ball or to at least obstruct the fielder's vision. A late slide will also help to block the fielder's sighting of the ball.

On the other hand, if it appears that the first toss will beat the runner easily, then a reversal must be made. If the player who has just completed the throw is slow in moving out of the baseline, then the runner should definitely try to make contact with him so as to draw an obstruction call. The important thing is that there be some reasoning in the runner's decision either to make a try for the next base immediately or to attempt one or more reversals in the base path.

★★★

Drills and method of instruction for Chapter 6 may be found on pages 158–69.

★★★

7

Advancing from Second Base to Third

Being a runner on second means being in scoring position. It means that not only was the runner successful enough at the plate to get to first, but also that he was able to find a way of advancing to second. He has made the defense aware of him, and they must be feeling some pressure. It is important now that he continue to demonstrate smart baserunning along with daring, too, should the chance present itself. He can't allow himself to curl into a shell and hide. His advancement and run are needed, and he shouldn't be satisfied until he has done everything he can to cross the plate before the inning ends.

Aggressiveness at second base begins with a good leadoff and the anticipation of scoring on a base hit. It also means looking for the passed ball or wild pitch as well as a possible tag-up after a fly ball.

Daring baserunning might also include the unexpected steal of third, especially off a walking lead when poor defense on the part of either the pitcher or infielders fails to keep a close check on the runner.

Smart baserunning at second starts with an attempt to read the catcher's signals and then flash them back to the batter through a prearranged signal system. The runner will also be psyched to score on a hit. He will angle out when coming around third and will anticipate the coach's arm gesture to continue home rather than thinking of stopping. Very important, too, will be the runner's knowledge of just when to come or stay on a ground ball hit to short or third. So many runners either fail to advance or get cut down needlessly on this kind of ground ball. There is no hard-and-fast rule, of course, because a number of different situations could present themselves. The number of outs is also a very important factor as well as the type and direction of the ground ball. Study and practice are a must if a team wants to capitalize on this play consistently. Nowhere are the opposites of daring and foolhardiness more aptly seen than on this play.

Remember that only at second base is the runner a full 90 feet away from a coach. Except for the occasional set-up steal sign flashed by the coach, that runner is pretty much on his own, and he had better be smart enough to handle it!

BEFORE STEPPING OFF THE BAG

1   Look to the third-base coach for a possible sign. Even with a play in the works, don't turn from the coach until he has completed all of his sign-giving. Otherwise, the defense will more easily pick off his signs.

2   Be certain that the pitcher has the ball before stepping off the base.

3   Try to recall any other pickoff plays that may have occurred earlier in the game as well as the routine used by the shortstop and second baseman in holding the runner close.

4   Be aware that your third-base coach will be watching your leadoff and will be calling out instructions to increase or decrease that leadoff as the infielders close in or move away.

LEADOFFS

The length of the leadoff should be as far as the shortstop unless, of course, the second baseman is positioned an even closer distance to the bag. Remember that the pitchers are encouraged to throw to second whenever they see daylight between the runner and the shortstop. If the runner is not stealing, a long leadoff isn't necessary anyway since the secondary lead should bring the runner to a point about 20 feet off the bag. The runner's primary lead need only be about four to five steps.

There are pros and cons that must be weighed in each situation in choosing between the straight-line versus the belly-deep leadoff. The straight-line is advised in steal situations as well as for any pitch for which the batter is given the take sign. This leadoff places the runner slightly closer to third, certainly an important factor when it is anticipated that the defense may be looking for a putout at third. Where no play is anticipated at third, the runner may prefer the belly-deep lead so as to be in better position to round third following a hit.

The runner at second is guided in his leadoff by the words of the third-base coach, who advises him regarding the moves of the shortstop behind him. Meanwhile, the runner keeps his eyes on the pitcher. In this situation, the first-base coach tries not to confuse the runner by calling out instructions. Getting help from the third-base coach is sufficient.

Teams should have a relay system worked out for use between the runner at second and the batter. Even with a runner at second, some catchers continue to use a single set of fingers for a particular pitch rather than a multiple set. When this occurs, the runner should have one signal set aside to indicate that a fast ball has been called and another for an off-speed pitch. The runner should never try to guess the pitch. If the runner doesn't get a good look at a certain pitch or just isn't sure, he lets that pitch be delivered without giving a signal. When relaying the signal, however, the runner must be careful to be very subtle. Otherwise, the catcher will soon realize what is happening and make some quick changes.

Whenever the runner notices a definite delay in the pitcher as he comes set, he should be on the lookout for a pickoff attempt.

Whenever the runner finds the shortstop running him back to the bag and then cutting in front of him as he starts his return to his position, the runner should again beware the pickoff attempt. The shortstop is momentarily trying to block the vision of the runner while the second baseman darts for the bag to take the pickoff throw.

STEALING THIRD BASE

A prearranged verbal signal should be understood between the coach and his players in the event that he sees the runner being poorly watched at second. Such a signal would tell the runner to steal third on that pitch.

A two-out, two-strike count situation in a noncrucial point in the ball game is one where the odds on a steal of third would be with the runner.

A good time to attempt a steal of third is whenever the pitcher allows the runner to assume a walking lead. This often occurs when inexperienced pitchers fail to give the runner more than a single look from the set position.

The leadoff on a steal of third should take place four to five steps off the bag, but directly in the baseline with the runner's heels aligned with the front edge of the base.

SPECIAL STEALS OF THIRD

The runner takes a very long secondary lead as the pitch is thrown. The catcher, knowing that he has got the runner picked off, throws down to second hurriedly. At this point the runner breaks for third. He stands a good chance of making it since the throw is long and no prearranged cut by the pitcher will be coming. A left-handed batter adds further to the chances of success for this play. Of course, the runner must have quick reflexes. Sometimes, too, the runner may find himself caught off the bag accidentally as a result of overaggressiveness. By first faking hard back toward second, he can diminish the chances of the catcher's running out toward him before throwing. It is a good idea to use this ploy even when the special play is on.

Another special steal of third involves the runner's intentionally getting picked off by a right-handed pitcher's move. It is very risky, though, and should be attempted only with very fast runners and only when playing with a comfortable lead. Of course, the runner's lead must be a long one, and his initial move to third comes the instant the pitcher begins his pickoff move. The runner is banking on the hope that the pitcher will go through with his throw to second even though the runner is running toward third at the time. The smart pitcher will usually not go through with the throw. The rules, remember, do allow for a fake throw to second. A rundown would then result. Yet, if the pitcher does throw to second, the play can catch the infielders off guard and this unique steal of third can become a reality.

ADVANCING ON A SACRIFICE BUNT

The runner responds to a sacrifice bunt as if he were at first, remembering, though, that a play at third will require a tag. It is crucial to time the second step of the secondary lead not with the contact of the bat and ball on the bunt, but with the *result* of the contact a split second later, so that the runner doesn't find himself breaking toward third on a popped-up bunt.

THE BUNT-AND-STEAL

This play calls for stealing third while the batter places a bunt in the direction of the third baseman. With no play to be made at third, the third baseman will have to go to first without checking the runner who, unknown to the fielder, has rounded the bag with every intention to continue home as the throw across the infield is made. The bunt must go to third to ensure the long throw and eventual two-base advance. Knowing that the first baseman will be attempting a return throw to the plate, the bunter slides into first. This way, he can delay or even prevent the first baseman from completing the play.

ADVANCING TO THIRD ON A GROUND BALL OR HIT

The runner must be aware of the third-base coach's four basic hand-and-arm signals to (1) slide, (2) keep going, (3) stop but take a turn and pick up sight of the ball, and (4) stop and hold the base.

On a ball hit to the left of the runner's leadoff position, advancement to third should always be made with two notable exceptions:

1 Advancement should not be attempted if the ball is stopped by the pitcher.

2   Advancement should not be attempted on a grounder hit be-
    tween the runner and the second-base bag if the shortstop is
    positioned there. This might occur with a strong left-handed
    hitter at the plate.

On a ball hit to the shortstop:

1   Advance to third (a) with two outs; (b) if the ball goes through
    into the outfield; (c) if the ball is a slow roller that must be
    charged and fielded on the infield grass.
2   Advance to third (after the throw) if the shortstop is forced to
    go deep in the hole for the ball. Try to take as great a lead as
    possible to cut down the distance to third. Yet remain close
    enough to second to prevent a possible pickoff toss by the short-
    stop.
3   Remain at second on a routine ground ball with less than two
    outs. Move back a few steps toward second so as to be in a
    straight line between the shortstop and the bag to make a throw
    there more difficult.

On a ball hit to the third baseman:

1   Advance to third (a) if the ball goes through into the outfield;
    (b) if the ball is a slow roller that must be charged and fielded
    on the infield grass; (c) if the ball sends the third baseman deep
    into the hole (after fielding the ball, he would be unable to re-
    turn to the bag in time for a tag of the runner); (d) if the ball is
    fielded over the line from a very deep position. (Again, he
    would be unable to return in time for a tag.)
2   Advance to third (after the throw) (a) on a routine ground ball
    thrown to first with two outs (the third baseman shouldn't be
    allowed the luxury of a third out here without a throw which
    could go astray); (b) if the ball is fielded from a deep position.
    (It would then take two long throws to get the runner. In both
    of these situations, the runner should place himself in exact line
    through which a pickoff throw would be made. However, no
    retreat from the leadoff position should be taken unless the
    throw is made or unless the runner is at least checked with a
    look or fake throw.)
3   Remain at second if a routine ground ball is hit with less than
    two outs unless the fielder makes no attempt to look the runner
    back to second. However, he usually will. If an attempted
    pickoff is made, the runner must be sure to be in a direct line

between the fielder at second base and the third baseman. Usually, the third baseman will decide against such a throw if he doesn't have a clear view of the man to whom he's throwing the ball.

APPROACHING THIRD ON A GROUND BALL OR HIT

1 Watch and listen to the third-base coach for his arm signals.

2 If the runner has a deep leadoff when the ball was hit, rounding third sharply will be easy. If the lead was taken directly in the baseline, a slight angling out will have to be made if the signal is to continue home. The angling technique is similar to the method performed when rounding first or second.

3 On a single, be psyched to score! Think in terms of rounding third under control and in stride. Think of returning to the bag only if signalled to do so. Don't think negatively, that is, of advancing to third but continuing only if signalled to do so. This only works to slow down the runner and works against the aggressiveness that runners should be attempting so hard to instill in themselves.

TAGGING UP ON A FLY BALL

The sprinter's stance is one technique used. From this position, the runner waits, listens, and watches for a visual arm signal from the coach. The more conventional method, though, places the responsibility for leaving at the proper moment with the runner. He stands with one foot on the bag while watching the ball enter the outfielder's glove. Actually, the foot is braced against the side of the bag for a better pushoff. He stands sideways facing the outfield except in the case of a ball hit to right field. The procedure here is to face the infield while watching the right fielder make the catch.

Depending upon the depth of the fly ball and the strength of the outfielder's arm, the procedure to follow usually should be:

1 *Shallow Fly Balls.* The odds of advancing are slim. Instead, the runner must hope that the outfielder either doesn't catch up to it or commits an error. Consequently, he goes about one-third of the distance to third, stops, and watches. Actually, the

strength of the outfielder's arm as well as the location of the ball will dictate the allowable distance from the base. Because he has time, the runner should be certain to be in a deep position in case the ball drops and the coach waves him home.

2 *Routine Fly Balls.* With the odds strongly in favor of a catch by the outfielder, the aggressive runner will tag up and fake a break to third in the hope that he may force a wild throw into a dead-ball area. However, the fake must be made to look legitimate to create the pressure necessary to rattle the outfielder sufficiently. When a runner moves down the line and awaits the outcome, his only chance of advancing comes if the outfielder drops an easy fly. But by tagging and faking an advance, there always exists the possibility of drawing a wild throw.

3 *Long Fly Balls.* With the exception of a fly ball to straightaway left field, the aggressive runner should tag at second and attempt to advance. Foul fly balls down the right-field line are no exception. Even if it is a shallow foul fly, the runner will often be able to advance. One factor making this possible is the element of surprise. The other is the fact that the ball will often be caught by the infielder with his back to the infield. These advantages can easily place the odds with the runner.

★★★

Drills and methods of instruction for Chapter 7 may be found on pages 169–71.

★★★

8

The Last 90 Feet to the Plate

Perched on third, the runner now realizes that he is 75 percent of the way toward his objective, because the goal of every runner should be to score. That's the name of the game.

While there still exists a number of special techniques to be learned, this advancement, nonetheless, should not be quite as complex as from the other bases. There are many advantages on the side of the runner here. First, he is close to his coach for any necessary interchange of important strategy. Next, he is assured that 90 feet is the most that he will have to run. He won't have to make any judgments about whether or not to advance beyond the next base. Nor will the runner need to consider any angling out to round the base nor the problem of overrunning or oversliding the base. Also, with the steal of home as rare a play as it is, good leadoffs are less of a problem. Pickoff attempts by the pitcher are also seldom seen and very rarely successful. Finally, with two outs, the runner is pretty well assured that the infield will attempt to get their third out at first and certainly not at the plate.

Although the runner at third seems to be less hampered with pickoff throws, his leadoff and consequential break to the plate as the ball is hit (with less than two outs) is the play that stands as one of the biggest challenges to the aggressive runner. This is because the daring team often has its runners on third attempt to score on ground balls even with the infield drawn in. Then, too, there are the squeeze plays to be learned, and again, it is the timing of the break to the plate that will most often spell the difference between success and failure. The timing of the break is also extremely important in stealing home which, while rare, can be far more successful when attempted with some commonsense guidelines in mind.

There is also technique to be learned in the art of tagging up following a caught fly ball. And, of course, the aggressive runner is always looking for the unexpected chance to score.

In reality, the greatest challenge facing this runner is the avoidance of any complacency over his enviable position. He must remember that until those final 90 feet of real estate are covered successfully, his ultimate goal as a runner has not been achieved.

LEADOFFS

1   Note the infield depth and any particular instructions from the third-base coach.

2   Assume a lead equal to the distance between the third baseman and the bag plus one step.

3   Take the lead in foul territory in the event that a hard-hit ball comes your way.

4   From the leadoff position, begin a walking lead toward home as soon as the pitcher commits himself to throw home (Fig. 8-1). The walking lead should consist of three steps (right-left-right) timed to arrive on the second right-foot step as the ball crosses the plate. In this way, the runner's body is still in forward motion as the ball is hit. Assuming that the runner has the go-ahead to attempt to score on a ground ball, he can already be in motion far down the baseline as the ball heads toward an infielder. Unless the ball is hit to the pitcher, the runner's chances of scoring are excellent.

5   Faking a steal of home can indeed be disconcerting to a pitcher and could certainly help the batter with his battle of the count. However, several of these bluffs by the same runner is a bad idea because each time it is done, the runner must abandon the walking lead strategy and begin not only putting on the brakes

Figure 8-1 Leadoff at Third Base—The runner's leadoff in foul territory is followed by a right-left-right stepping movement while facing home. The final step is timed with the moment that the pitch will be crossing the plate.

(Figure 8-1 continued)

as the ball is delivered, but also must hurry to retreat to third.
He puts himself in a poor position to score should the ball get
away from the catcher and roll 5 to 15 feet. With the walking
lead, scoring on such a play would hold a great chance of success. This is because as the ball is rolling away from the catcher,
the runner finds himself moving toward home instead of back
to third.

6 If the pitch is not hit, the runner returns to third in fair territory so as to restrict the catcher's vision of the third baseman. In
addition, the runner continues to keep his eye on the catcher as
he returns to third. Of course, if the catcher is seen starting to
set himself for a pickoff throw, a rush for the bag and perhaps
a dive, too, will be necessary.

UNPLANNED CHANCES TO SCORE

1 Be ready to dash home on a wild throw back to the pitcher that
is not being backed up by an infielder.

2   Be ready to run home if the catcher goes out to talk to the pitcher without asking for time and without anyone left to guard the plate.

3   Trying to score on a wild pitch or passed ball with no outs is poor strategy unless the runner is quite sure of his chances. With one or two outs, the risk is lessened. However, the decision should be left to the runner, who will most likely have a better feel for his chances for success, certainly more so than his coach.

REACTING TO GROUND BALLS

On a ground ball hit to any infielder other than the pitcher, aggressive baserunning dictates that the runner attempt to score unless the situation has prompted the coach to tell him otherwise. With infielders playing deep or even halfway, there certainly shouldn't be much risk in trying to score. However, with the infield in, the aggressive team often will still force the defense to come up with the good play by trying to score. Remember that the walking lead and quick jump as the ball is hit do much to enhance the chances of scoring. This is just another way of heaping even more pressure on the defense. If in error the runner should make a break for the plate on a ball hit back to the pitcher, he should hold up and try to delay long enough in a rundown to give the batter-runner a chance to advance to second.

Even when playing conservatively and when the defense has the infield in, a runner on third should break for the plate after a throw to first by the third baseman. The runner certainly wouldn't have to retreat to third just because the third baseman glanced his way upon fielding the grounder. Then, too, there would be no one at the bag to take a throw anyway. Only if the runner were within reach of the third baseman might he be forced to retreat.

TAGGING UP ON A FLY BALL

Once the coach has told the runner to tag up and try to score, the runner handles the rest. That is, he is the one who decides just when the ball enters the outfielder's glove. His crouch is a slight one with one foot on the bag and the other in the baseline with the body facing the infield and his eyes on the outfielder making the catch. The crouch in the stance helps the runner produce a strong drive off the right leg. Many runners make the mistake of placing most of their body weight over the left leg. In so doing, they take their first step with the right foot, thus losing the benefit of a complete step. Instead, the weight should be concentrated over the right leg so that the first step is actually taken with the left leg.

Even when the coach advises against the attempt of a runner to score, the runner might still like to fake a break in hopes of producing a wild throw.

Tag up on any fly ball that appears catchable, including foul flies, sinking liners, and deep pop-ups chased by infielders with their backs to the infield. If any of these drop in, especially the sinking liners, the chances of scoring are excellent.

After tagging up and starting down the line following a fly to right field, the runner uses his own judgment to stop and return. This occurs when he sees an excellent throw he thinks will beat him.

On a foul fly deep to the catcher, tag up and be ready to attempt to score if the defense fails to cover the plate.

Whenever a throw to the plate is coming from behind the runner, he must listen to and watch for the arm signal of the on-deck batter. He will be stationed in foul territory just to the inside of the third-base line, but deep enough into foul territory to be out of the way of the play. His signal will be one of two: hands-up or hands-down.

STEALING HOME

Ideally, the play is attempted with two outs, but with less than two strikes on the batter. The steal may come against a right-handed pitcher, but a left-hander is preferred since his back is to the runner while he is winding up. It is mandatory that the pitcher use the full windup since the runner will need approximately $3\frac{1}{2}$ seconds to cover the distance from his leadoff position to home plate. Since the pitcher's fast ball will require about half a second to reach the plate, he must use about 3 seconds in his windup if the runner is to have a chance. The runner can also help himself by getting a leadoff that will leave a distance that he can cover in less than $3\frac{1}{2}$ seconds. It helps if the third baseman is lax in holding the runner fairly close.

The runner examines his chances of success by first performing a trial run. He travels as far down the line as possible, while still being able to get back. On this trial run, his eyes are kept on the pitcher.

There is a definite advantage in beginning the actual break-off of a walking lead even if it means giving up a bit of the leadoff distance to do so.

In telling his secrets of stealing home as many times as he did, the great Rogers Hornsby said that he always wanted the batter swinging, but swinging high to miss the ball. The idea was to keep the catcher back, busy, and distracted. For very obvious safety reasons, few advocate that method today. However, much the same objective can be accomplished by having the batter assume both a deep and crowded position at the plate. The deep positioning will keep the catcher a bit farther from the front edge of the plate. The batter's crowding of the plate will help to block slightly the catcher's view of the runner. Of course, the batter must be right-handed to accomplish either of these objectives.

It is imperative that the batter have the signal. In fact, there should be an acknowledgment signal back to the coach. When the pitch does come in, the batter shouldn't be in any hurry to back out of the box unless he gets brushed back.

While a few coaches advocate the head-first slide on a steal of home, most prefer the feet-first slide. Actually, the head-first slide would provide a smaller tag area for the catcher. Furthermore, if done well, the catcher would have little time to move up for a block of the plate. However, this is something that the runner just doesn't know when he begins his move to the plate. As a consequence, sliding feet first is considered the safer method. Besides, it provides the runner with a chance to knock the ball out of the catcher's mitt should he not get home in time.

THE SQUEEZE PLAY

There are three types of squeeze plays: the suicide, safety, and sacrifice. Because none represents a steal of home, the timing of the break to the plate is different.

With the suicide squeeze, the runner breaks as the pitcher's arm is coming forward. By this time, it is too late for the pitcher to throw high and tight. Of course, it is extremely important that the batter get wood on the ball even if the pitch is out of the strike zone. About the only exception would be the pitch in the dirt. Otherwise, failure to make contact dooms the play to failure. At best, the runner might be able to brake in enough time to at least necessitate a rundown. However, if the ball is bunted as planned, the runner will score easily.

The safety or delayed squeeze is both more and less risky at the same time. With this play, the runner doesn't break to the plate until he sees the ball bunted successfully. The batter is not compelled to go after a bad pitch. If the pitch, then, is taken, the runner is able to return to third easily. On the other hand, the runner could indeed be put out at the plate if the ball was bunted sharply and directly at the pitcher or at one of the charging infielders. The more aggressive teams and runners tend to prefer the suicide squeeze unless the game situation dictates otherwise.

The sacrifice squeeze is a unique form of squeeze. It is used less frequently than its counterparts mainly because it is less known among coaches. In addition, a bunter with very good bat control is required. The play is best used when the third baseman is already playing a shortened position in anticipation of a squeeze. The batter *must* get his bunt to the third baseman. The runner at first reacts as he would to any sacrifice bunt, breaking for second only when the ball is put down. In his leadoff and even as the ball is bunted, the runner at third remains *behind* the third baseman, who will be anticipating a runner streaking toward home. When no such runner appears in his vision, he will be forced to go to first as he often would with a sacrifice bunt. In doing so, he will be unable to check the runner at third, who will be just a couple steps behind him.

Of course, the runner could still be thrown out at the plate with a good return throw from the first baseman. However, in anticipation of such an attempted relay, the batter-runner helps by sliding into first just as if he were trying to break up a double play. The play stands little chance of success if the ball is bunted anywhere else since (1) the fielder will have time to check the runner at third, (2) the runner will be unable to cheat as much on his lead while the ball is being charged, and (3) the throw to first will be much shorter.

SPECIAL DELAYED STEAL PLAY

Following an earlier signal from the coach, the batter, upon receiving a walk, breaks at full speed toward second as soon as he reaches first. As the surprised pitcher commits himself to a throw to second, the runner at third breaks for the plate. It is important for the batter-runner to run toward second at full speed. In this way, the pitcher has little time, if any, to check the runner at third, who will be increasing his lead as he prepares to make his break. Otherwise, the runner at third, upon being looked or faked back to the bag, must wait for the first throw of the rundown before breaking. This will decrease the chances of success since everyone will then have in mind the intentions of the runner at third as the rundown ensues. Making the break, though, as a rundown toss is made from a middle infielder to a left-handed first baseman isn't a bad idea. For the left-handed first baseman, the pivot to home is more difficult and time-consuming than for his right-handed counterpart.

★★

Drills and methods of instruction for Chapter 8 may be found on pages 171–74.

★★

9

Multiple-Runner Situations and Strategies

For the aggressive-minded team, finding two or three runners on base is like awaiting New Year's Eve or the Fourth of July. Unless the team is forced to play conservatively because of the score or inning, the multiple-runner situation presents numerous opportunities for skilled and strategic baserunning. This kind of pressure will force the defense into mistakes that may produce runs and will increase the morale of the offense.

Think about it. With no one on base, the defense can concentrate on good positioning and can zero in their efforts on the batter. The pitcher can place all his concentration into his battle with the batter.

With one runner on base, the defense is faced with a distraction. The runner's presence can force infielders to play out of their usual positions in guarding against bunt or steal possibilities. A pitch that gets away from the catcher will probably result in an advancement. Pitchers must throw from the stretch to guard against long leadoffs and steals. The concentration of every member of the defense becomes split between two people.

Now, consider that scenario extended to include a second or even a third runner. Filled with confidence and intent on demonstrating their skills at the drop of a signal, these runners will be sure to pressure the defense when the chance arises. The sky's the limit! There are a total of four multiple-runner combinations, the first and third situation being by far the most intriguing. While teams may find all the described plays too numerous to include in their playbook, certainly the mastery of a number of them will keep the defense guessing. There is no reason, for example, why the offense must run a first and third double steal the same way twice even if the situation presents itself many times during the game.

Lecturing the team on the mechanics of each play is not sufficient, though, for mastering the necessary techniques. The coach and players must be willing to pay the price through the kind of hard practice and drill needed for success. Then, each successful execution of a baserunning strategy will only increase the team's desire to try another. Even a baserunning blunder will cause the team to want to discuss the play in practice to determine what went wrong and how to correct it. The fact that a play failed will only make it an even bigger challenge for the future. In a phrase, "When the running gets tough, the tough get running."

RUNNERS ON FIRST AND SECOND

General Reminders

The runner at second should lead off in the baseline with less than two outs, or with two outs whenever the take sign is on for the batter. In addition, a straight leadoff is always in order whenever a bunt or a steal strategy is on. Otherwise, the runner bellies-out two or three steps toward the outfield as the leadoff is taken.

The belly-out lead provides the runner with a better angle for rounding third if the batter responds with a hit to the outfield. With the straight leadoff, the runner is placing himself slightly closer to third in anticipation that the defense will be trying to make a play there. In most cases, this would certainly be the case with any bunt or steal strategy. A straight leadoff is also helpful if a wild pitch or passed ball occurs. If the ball is hit through the infield while the runner is in a straight leadoff, the runner merely angles out when approaching third as he would at any other base.

Both runners must be especially alert for the possibility of pickoff plays at their base. Well-trained teams look upon this situation as one of the most favorable for a pickoff play at one base or another.

On catchable fly balls to medium depth or deep left field, the resulting throw-in will be in the direction of third base. The runner at second might wish to tag up and advance, the same as if he were a lone runner. With the entire play in front of him, the runner at first should also tag and strongly consider an advance if he sees the lead runner try for third. The chance for such advancement from first to second is far more difficult and risky on flies to center and right, since the throws back toward the infield usually are in the direction of second base.

The Sacrifice Bunt

Executed with less than two outs, this play will result in an out at first, but with two runners instead of one now in scoring position.

With one exception, the strategy and mechanics for both the batter and runners are the same as with the regular sacrifice bunt with a lone runner at first. That exception should be an attempt by the batter to bunt the ball toward the third baseman. Making the third baseman field the bunt will force the defensive shortstop to cover third if there is any intention of getting a force play at that base. This defensive play is not difficult for the well-trained team, but can cause fits for many others, especially those whose infielders fail to communicate to each other regarding coverage plans prior to the play.

The Double Steal

Because of the risk involved, and because the offense already has one runner in scoring position, this play is best used when ahead in the game. In addition, a pitcher who carelessly holds the runner on second helps to eliminate much of the risk for the offense. The same is true for careless infielders.

There is one important point for the runner at first to remember. Because the pitcher could step off the rubber or could in some other way upset the runner's break at second, the lead runner might wisely decide not to give himself up as an easy out at third. Consequently, the runner at first must pick up sight of the runner at second as the pitcher goes to the plate with the ball. If the lead runner is seen breaking for third, the back runner also goes. If the lead runner doesn't go, neither does the back runner. When running, though, the back runner must run hard in anticipation of a possible overthrow at third.

The Double-Steal—Fake-Bunt Variation

On this surprise play, the batter squares to bunt as both runners break. The fake bunt will pull in the third baseman while simultaneously taking him out of position to receive the catcher's throw. The play gambles on the acting ability of the batter as well as noncommunication between the third baseman and shortstop. If either gamble fails, someone will be there to receive the throw. In that case, the chances of success for the play are reduced to those of the regular double steal.

The surprise effect is best achieved by performing the play on the first pitch.

The Double-Steal—Fake-Bunt and Slash-Hit Variation

As in the previous play, action begins with the batter squaring to bunt. However, at the last second, the batter draws back the bat to take the pitch. If the defense wasn't prepared before, it certainly will be now. The defense decided upon, it is hoped, will find the shortstop moving away from his normal position, probably toward third as the third baseman charges. As the second pitch comes in, the runners break. The batter, who again has assumed a bunting position, this time draws back the bat and takes a cut at the ball. The hope is that he will be able to punch it past the drawn-in third baseman or through the vacated shortstop area. Most definitely, the batter should swing to protect the runners, even if it may mean going after a not-so-good pitch. If the pitch is missed, the play reduces to that of a regular double steal with the defense possibly caught out of position to take the throw at third. If the play results in a ground ball that is fielded, at least both runners will advance.

When breaking, both runners must catch sight of the batter in case the ball is popped-up.

It is important to try to hit the ball to the left side of the infield where the infielders are moving. Therefore, the play is best attempted with a right-handed batter.

The Double-Steal—Pickoff-at-First Variation

Used only with less than two outs, this double-steal variation requires very fast runners on both bases. Furthermore, it should be tried only with the offense in the lead.

The runner at first assumes a casually long leadoff. He tries not to give the impression of being daring, but rather of being careless. Since the pitcher or catcher may not spot this long lead-off before the first pitch, the batter may have to take the first pitch. In fact, if the first pitch is a ball, he also could afford to take a second pitch.

Within the first two pitches, however, it is expected that either the pitcher or catcher will attempt a pickoff at first. In either case, both runners take off for the next base as soon as they see the play being made. If the first baseman tries for the putout at third base, it will take a hard and accurate throw to get the runner there. Remember, the runner at second, like the one at first, is very fast to begin with and also has anticipated the pickoff. If the runner does arrive safely, it means that the runner from first has been able to advance also. If the throw goes toward second base instead, the runner from first uses his quickness and speed to stop and remain in a rundown as long as necessary for the lead runner to attempt to break home.

This shouldn't be quite as difficult as it may sound, since the runner from second will be arriving at third by the time the first baseman's throw is arriving at second. If a throw is made to the plate, the back runner can easily scamper to second to be in scoring position no matter what happens to the lead runner. This is not a play for average-speed runners or for coaches who are faint of heart.

RUNNERS ON SECOND AND THIRD

General Reminders

The runner at second must always know how the front runner has been instructed to react to a ground ball or fly ball. Only then will he be able to respond most efficiently.

Unless a steal or bunt play is on, the runner at second can assume a belly-deep lead since a wild pitch or passed ball might produce a play at the plate, but not one at third.

Single-Squeeze or Double-Squeeze Bunt

Both plays are attempted with less than two outs and a capable bunter at the plate.

The play is a daring one and is sure to catch the defensive players by surprise. Seldom will they expect to see the ball laid down with two runners already in scoring position.

The play may be called for any of the following reasons:

1   A run is needed badly.
2   The batter is a very good bunter.
3   The batter often pops the ball up or strikes out.
4   The coach feels that the defense is not prepared to handle a bunt due to a poor fielding, lackadaisical, or untrained team.
5   The offense is ahead in the score, but the coach is looking to inject even more aggressiveness into his running game. If successful, the play is always sure to boost team morale.

While a single squeeze play can be executed as either a suicide or delayed squeeze, the double squeeze requires the suicide variety. In this case, the runner at third does his best not to tip off his intentions to the pitcher. He takes a safe lead and only breaks for the plate when the pitcher's leg begins to come forward. At this point, the back runner also breaks for the next base. If the ball is bunted to anyone other than the third baseman, the short throw to first will force this play to remain a single squeeze.

However, it should be the batter's intention to make the charging third baseman field the ball. With no play to be had at the plate, the third baseman may turn to check the runner who has just rounded third. If he does so, the runner there will have to break stride and be content with his one-base advance. However, if no check is made on this runner, he continues to the plate without breaking stride. If the return throw to the plate from the first baseman gets the runner, one run will have still scored, perhaps one that wouldn't have been notched had the batter been allowed to swing away. If the runner gets in safely, two runs will have scored due to the team's baserunning aggressiveness. Again, this is a play whereby a slide into first by the bunter can greatly hinder or even prevent the anticipated return throw by the first baseman.

The "Pickoff at Second" Steal

This is another daring play whose chances of success are slim on the higher levels of play but which can cause havoc with the less experienced. Strategically, it is best attempted with two outs and one or two strikes on the batter, unless that batter is one of the team's best.

As the pitch comes in, the runner at third moves as far down the line as safely possible. This time his lead is taken in fair territory. The batter takes the pitch unless there are two strikes. The runner from second momentarily pretends to forget that third is occupied as he heads for third in a sprint as if stealing. Halfway there, he puts on the brakes as hard as possible as he hears his coach calling out for him to go back. He does, indeed, try to return to second. As he does so, he watches for and hopefully draws a throw from the catcher. It is very important that this runner sprint back toward second. Otherwise, the catcher may have sufficient time to check the runner at third before throwing.

As the throw is made to second, the front runner breaks for the plate. The runner returning to second then stops in his tracks and is content to get in a diversionary rundown if he feels that he cannot return safely. If the infielder, upon receiving the throw, relays the ball back home, the back runner moves either to second or third. If the defense goes for the out on the rundown, the runner in that rundown must be certain to remain "alive" long enough for the run to score in case there are two outs at the time.

RUNNERS ON FIRST AND THIRD

General Reminders

The runner on third should always break for the plate on any ground ball that appears to have double play written on it. If the defense instead goes for the out at the plate, the runner, unless he has a good chance of scoring, stops quickly. He tries to remain in a rundown until the two back runners have had a chance to move up to first and second and maybe even to second and third.

On any double-steal play, the runner at third moves directly into the baseline as he assumes his leadoff rather than in foul territory. This will make it more difficult for the catcher to make a throw there. He will have greater trouble spotting the third baseman and will be more wary of hitting the runner.

Double-Advancement Plays

This play will work against all but the most highly trained teams. Unfortunately, the circumstances needed to make the play work will seldom present themselves over the course of the season. With runners on first and third and less than two outs, a pop-up must be hit either to the catcher, the first baseman in foul territory or in short right field, or to the right fielder in short to medium right field.

In all of these cases, the ball has not been hit far enough to allow the runner at third to tag and advance. However, with this play, both runners are alerted by their respective coaches to return to their bases in anticipation of tagging up and advancing. The runner at third then moves down the line as far as possible without being in danger of a throw to his base. Meanwhile, the runner at first breaks for second as the catch is made. He tries to keep his eye on the ball, and if a throw is made to get him, he stops and gets in a rundown. If the infielder receiving the ball relays the ball to the plate, the back runner moves up to second base. As the throw is made to get the advancing back runner, the runner at third breaks for the plate. The relay home will always be late unless the defense utilizes the pitcher as the cut man. This is the one correct way to defense this stunt. If the runner at third anticipates such a cut, he may be wise only to fake the advance and be content to see the back runner advance to second.

Although a team cannot anticipate just when this play will present itself, the play must be drilled in practice so that all players will know just what is required of them when the time comes.

Safety-Squeeze Bunt

A safety squeeze with runners at first and third can score an easy run and set up another runner in scoring position at second or third. It is best used in a close game or even early in a game to get on the scoreboard. While it should be attempted with less than two outs, working the play with nobody out is ideal.

A less-than-good bunter is what will usually dictate the use of the safety squeeze rather than the suicide variety.

The batter doesn't try to hide his intentions. He attempts to bunt only a good pitch, and he attempts to bunt toward the charging third baseman. In fact, he must bunt it there if the runner on first is to have any chance of advancing to third. While the runner at first makes his break when he sees the ball laid down, the runner at third doesn't. He delays his break until the third baseman throws to first. All the while he has been slowly creeping down the third-base line as the third baseman has been charging in to field the ball. In all likelihood, the third baseman will not have time to check the whereabouts of the runner.

Obviously, then, it is extremely important for the ball to be handled by no one else, since a pitcher or catcher, with more time and a shorter throw, will cause the runner at third to hold while the putout is made at first. If the ball is bunted to third as planned, the back runner continues in full stride around second and continues to third. If the first baseman does try to make a play, it most likely will take the form of a relay back to the plate rather than the much longer throw to third.

The runner at first should not attempt a steal on this play. He should be patient in waiting for the bunt to be put down successfully. One reason is that a popped-up bunt would result in a double play. Second, although a steal might give the back runner an even better chance of advancing to third, what good would it do if the ball were bunted to someone other than the third baseman? The runner at third would have only to hold his base and the back runner would have to stop at second.

Suicide-Squeeze Bunt

This play is riskier than the safety-squeeze variety since it could easily result in a double play or even a triple play if the bunt is popped-up. On the other hand, successful execution results in a sure run and, most likely, a two-base advancement by the runner at first.

While bunting toward third is still preferred, it is not a must. The only must is that the batter make contact and get the bunt on the ground away from the plate. If that occurs, the runner at third can be just an average runner and still score easily since he will have plenty of time. As with the usual suicide play, the runner breaks as the pitcher's leg begins its movement toward the plate. The runner at first also breaks at the same time so that he will give no premature signal to the defense that any play is on. A poorly placed bunt could hold the back runner to a one-base advance. However, a bunt to third should provide for a two-base advance unless the third baseman is able to check him before throwing to first.

The Hit-and-Run

Very similar to the regular hit-and-run play, this one is even better. Normally, the break by the runner at first will find one of the infielders moving toward second to take a throw from the catcher. However, because the defense will be suspecting the double steal, both infielders will be moving toward second, one to take a possible throw and the other in an attempt to cut the throw and relay to the plate. This means that 50 percent of the infield will be opening up for the batter to punch the ball through. If that does happen, the back runner will be able to advance to third. Of course, on the pitch, the runner on third takes his normal leadoff but doesn't break home until he sees the ball hit someplace other than in the air. Even if the ball is hit on the ground to the pitcher, he is smarter to break for the plate than to allow the defense to turn a double play at second and first. If he sees that he is going to be a sure out at the plate as the throw is coming home, he gets himself in a rundown while the runner from first tries to advance to third if the rundown can be made to last long enough.

A good contact hitter who can hit to the opposite field is really needed here, but the contact itself is more important than hitting to the opposite field since portions of both sides of the infield will open for the batter.

In case the pitch is not hit, the runner at third must have prior instructions from the coach as to what his reaction is expected to be if a throw is made to second. Should he fake a break and return to protect the back runner, or should he react by breaking for the plate? He must know. The instructions of the coach will surely depend on the running abilities of the runner at third as well as the score and inning.

The Fake Double Steal of Second

This play might be used when the runner at third lacks quickness or when the defense has been observed to be very aggressive and quick in making the cut and relay. Yet, by a successful execution, a second runner can be placed in scoring position.

The runner at first breaks as he would for any steal and runs directly for the bag. If the take sign has not been given to the batter, then this runner will have to give a look in on his way to second. Meanwhile, the runner at third must convincingly fake a break for the plate. So as not to find himself too far down the line and unable to return safely, his leadoff should be shortened by two steps. The fake run should consist of a hard right-left-right series of steps. It is intended to be convincing enough to cause the defense to cut the throw down to second. If the throw is not cut, the back runner could be in trouble unless he gets a good jump on his break. If the cut is made, the front runner may find a play being made on him, thus requiring a dive back into third.

Because the defense will allow the ball to go through to get the runner with two outs, the play should be attempted only with less than two outs.

The Double Steal

Strategically, this play should be attempted when the offense is trying to get across the tying or winning run late in the game. But again, the lower the level of play, the more unprepared the defenses are to handle this play successfully. As a consequence, the play can often work to the benefit of the offense in many situations other than just close ball games in late innings.

On the pitch, which the batter is instructed to take, the runner at first breaks for second and picks up sight of the ball as he nears the bag. If the throw has the runner beaten and there are two outs, the runner stops, backtracks, and remains in any rundown long enough for the first runner to score. If the throw by the catcher is immediately relayed back home instead, then the back runner merely moves up to second base. With less than two outs, the coach's philosophy may be to handle everything the same way.

However, there is also merit to the ploy of having the back runner go directly into second whether the throw has him beaten or not. The idea here is that any tag applied to that runner will give the front runner additional time to beat a subsequent relay back home. Also, if the runner at third was faked back to the bag, the runner approaching second might still be able to arrive safely if he slides straight in rather than holding up for what will be a sure out in the rundown. Of course, the catcher's throw could go to third or back to the pitcher, in which case the back runner will easily be able to move up.

The runner at third, knowing that the pitch will be taken and also aware that the catcher's throw could come to third, takes his usual leadoff, not in foul territory but in the baseline. As the pitch is delivered, the runner moves down the line only a safe distance from where he knows he would be able to return if the catcher decides to make a snap throw there. He must remember, too, that another option for the catcher is to make a complete fake (including the follow-through) to second before bringing the arm back again for a throw to third. Further, he must remember the old little-league ploy of having the pitcher cut off the throw to second and relay it to the third baseman. Of course, the play does have merit, so the runner must watch for that possibility.

Otherwise, the runner breaks for the plate the instant he thinks that the throw heading toward second is not going to be cut by the pitcher. Sometimes, the catcher will either look the runner back to third or fake a throw there. If that happens, the runner may find himself dashing back toward third or even diving in at a time that he otherwise would be breaking to the plate.

If the runner has gone straight to the base, then the thought of a double steal will have to be shelved. However, if the runner from first has allowed himself to be hung up in a rundown, then the front runner recovers, begins creeping down the line, and finally makes his break. His move should come when the defense has momentarily forgotten about him or when the defense is in a poor-throwing position. Such poor-throwing positions would include longer throws from the second-base area rather than shorter ones from the first-base area. Yet, if the first baseman is left-handed and just in the process of throwing toward second, he will have to make a difficult pivot before throwing home.

With any relay throw from an infielder back to the plate, the runner at second, if still alive, must be ever watchful and alert for a bad throw which might allow still further advancement to third.

The Delayed Double Steal

This play is designed to catch the defense sleeping. It is also a good play to call when it is suspected that the catcher might otherwise prefer to hold onto the ball rather than throwing through to second. If a run is needed, the offense can't be content to see only the back runner advance. It must try to make the catcher throw down. Whether it be for this reason or to catch the infielders or catcher unaware, the play begins with the back runner. Instead of breaking on the pitch, he takes a three-step secondary lead and then breaks. With the batter taking the pitch, the third step of the secondary lead will coincide closely with the moment that the catcher will be raising his arm to return the ball to the pitcher. Because the throw has a good chance of beating the runner, the back runner stops short of second, content to become involved in a rundown. Because of the runner's late start, a catcher who might otherwise hold the ball will now be more confident in throwing the ball to second.

Best used with a left-handed batter to cover up further the sight of the breaking runner, the delayed double steal is usually attempted with two outs.

As with the standard double steal, the runner at third takes his lead in the baseline and only breaks when he feels that the throw will not be cut off by the pitcher. If he is faked back to third, he will have to delay his break until an opportune moment during the resulting rundown near second.

The Double-Steal Walkoff Variation

Intended more than anything else to cause an inexperienced pitcher to balk, this is not a type of double steal to attempt against a well-disciplined defense. If no balk is committed, the runners will both have to do a lot of scrambling to produce a run.

The runner at first takes his normal lead and then, when not being watched but with the pitcher on the rubber, begins the first few steps of an actual walk toward second. It is hoped the sudden calling by the pitcher's teammates that the runner at first is going, will cause the pitcher to begin but not complete a pickoff throw when he no longer sees the runner there. That constitutes a balk and both runners would advance.

Another theory has the runner begin his walkoff just after the pitcher turns his head away from the runner. While this will give the runner a perfect walking lead, it might also wipe out the chances of a balk if the pitcher should immediately go from his look to first into his kick to the plate. What is most important is that the walk be started with the pitcher on the rubber and with the pitcher's eyes off the runner. If the pitcher smartly steps back off the rubber, thus becoming an infielder, the back runner will have to remain alive in the ensuing rundown until the front runner can make his break and score.

If no balk is committed, the runner at third will have to choose one of three or four opportunities to break depending on the moves of the defense. If the pitcher seems overly concerned with charging at the back runner without thought of the runner at third, then a break should be made immediately. If the pitcher's first throw is to the first baseman, then the front runner can creep down the line and break on the longer throw from the first baseman toward second. However, if the first throw is to the second baseman or shortstop, especially after a fake to third to drive the runner back, the front runner will have to break as the infielder at second throws back to the first baseman. This might be an opportunity to break if the first baseman is left-handed, since a 90-degree counterclockwise pivot is needed before he can throw home. Of course, there is always the possibility that one of the infielders will forget about the front runner in his attempt to get the putout in the rundown.

The Double-Steal Runoff Variation

In leaving first base for second, running off rather than walking off holds some advantages. In fact, it is the only difference between this play and the walkoff play. Running off is intended to gain two possible advantages over the other play. First, because of the greater surprise movement of the runner, the pitcher may become startled by the warning shouts of his teammates. Thus, the chances for a balk are increased. Secondly, by breaking into a sprint from the outset, the runner will force the pitcher to throw toward second without giving him time first to fake the lead runner back toward third. This should allow the front runner to gain a longer lead and better break if he does decide to break on the throw to second. Of course, the runner there will stop and try to remain in a rundown.

Again, the play is best attempted with two outs, perhaps a poor hitter at bat, and with a less experienced pitcher. However, against a smart pitcher this play still stands a slightly better chance of working than the walkoff.

The chances of a balk can be increased if the runner at third, seeing the runner at first break, also breaks simultaneously for about two steps. It will act as a momentary diversion against the right-handed pitcher. It might further confuse him, too, upon hearing that the runner is going and yet seeing the runner at third stop after his two steps and quickly return.

If two are out, the runner at first will be running hard but also will be watching over his shoulder for the throw. However, with less than two outs, the coach may wish the runner to go all the way to second, perhaps to be tagged out but creating a diversion to give the front runner more time for his run to the plate.

The Double-Steal Runoff Variation against a Left-Handed Pitcher

This is a very risky play that should be attempted only when in the lead. Yet, it can and often does work against an inexperienced left-handed pitcher. After coming set, the lefty will glance over his shoulder at third, then glance at the runner at first, and then pitch home. At the instant the pitcher is glancing at third, the runner at first breaks. Within a split second, the pitcher's head will be turning toward the runner at first. Within that time frame, the runner at third also breaks for the plate. Teammates will be yelling that the runner is going. The pitcher will think, "Yes, I know he's going. I can see that happening right in front of me, but I'll get him."

Of course, what he doesn't realize is that his teammates are referring to the front runner boldly breaking for the plate, not the back runner's dash for second. Often, by the time that this mistake is realized, the throw to the plate is too late and the runner going into second is safe, too. Also, the chance of a balk still exists, especially if the pitcher first has notions of throwing to first and then hesitates.

The Intentional-Pickoff Double Steal

Another risky play to be sure, the intentional-pickoff double steal can be quite successful when used with quick-reflexed runners against an inexperienced or poor-throwing, left-handed first baseman. A left-handed pitcher is also preferred, but not required. The play can be run with any number of outs. The left-handedness of the first baseman is also only a preference, not an absolute necessity.

The play begins as the runner at first notes whether the first baseman throws with the left or right arm. This may prove important later in the play. He then assumes a long lead as the pitcher begins his stretch. A pickoff attempt at first is needed for the play to work. At this point, the play opens into a number of possible variations.

One variation has the runner at third breaking for the plate as soon as the pitcher is seen committing himself to a pickoff attempt at first. If the pitcher instead goes through with the pitch and the catcher makes the pickoff attempt at first, then again the runner at third will break. The surprise break by the front runner as well as the left-handedness (if that be the case) of the first baseman are what the offense banks on for the success of this variation. With a left-handed pitcher, the runner at third will be able to take an even longer lead. If no pickoff is attempted, the runners must try again on the next pitch with a still longer lead at first.

The more popular scenario for this play finds the runner at third not breaking, but instead creeping slowly down the line as the first baseman, upon receiving the pickoff throw, proceeds to go after the advancing runner from first. If the first baseman throws across the infield to the third baseman, the front runner breaks for the plate as the back runner moves up to second. With two outs, the runner from first must continue to watch over his shoulder as he tries to remain in a rundown long enough for the front runner to break and score. That break will come when one of the fielders taking part in the rundown is in a poor throwing position.

One such time might be when the first baseman's pivot foot is extended toward second, especially if he's left-handed. With less than two outs, more time and more of a diversion is created for the front runner by having the back runner break into a sprint for second, hoping to draw a long and hurried throw. Not only should this benefit the runner at third, but should also enhance the chances of the back runner's arriving safely at second. Remember, the shortstop and second baseman will not have expected this break on the pickoff and may be late in starting for second to take the throw. Here, it is also important for the runner to remember whether the first baseman is left- or right-handed. He wants to slide into that side of the second-base bag that coincides with the side from which the first baseman throws. With a left-handed first baseman, then, the runner would be sliding into the left side of second, causing the thrower to aim the ball toward the right-field side. This could produce a temporary blind spot for the fielder, but would definitely make it difficult for him to apply the tag and come up throwing accurately to the plate.

Sliding toward the right-field side of the bag for a right-handed-throwing first baseman would cause problems, too. The right-handed fielder at second will have to take the throw to the inside of the base, make a sweeping tag, regain his balance, make a difficult clockwise pivot, and throw home. The chances are good, too, that the throw could hit the runner.

RUNNERS ON FIRST, SECOND, AND THIRD

General Reminders

While a bases-loaded situation certainly presents the greatest threat of all the multiple-runner possibilities, it ironically presents the offense with the fewest options as regards baserunning strategies. Hit-and-runs aren't possible. Suicide-squeeze bunts could result in double or even triple plays if the ball is popped-up. Safety squeezes could easily lead to a force play, and there is not much room for potential base stealers to roam. The one play that has been known to work, especially on the lower levels, is one form or another of a delayed triple steal inaugurated by an intentional pickoff.

All runners must be especially wary of pickoffs, particularly with the back runners.

The 3-2 count with two outs is an excellent time for the defense to attempt pickoffs since careless runners will often be thinking of getting an extra-good jump. Runners must be certain that the ball is going to the plate before breaking for the next base.

On the 3-2 count with two outs, the runner from third must not break too far down the line even though he may be safe from any pickoff. One reason is safety, of course, since it may be nearly impossible to avoid a line-shot hit his way. Furthermore, the runner who advances far down the line can be a great distraction to the hitter, who can see him through his peripheral vision.

The Delayed Triple Steal

This play is best attempted with two outs and a weak hitter at the plate.

The offense must effect a pickoff throw from the catcher against one of the back runners while the runner at third breaks home. Because the catcher will most likely be wary of throwing to second, the offense should instead concentrate its efforts on its runner at first. On the pitch he makes a fake break for second, but one that is about three steps beyond the usual fake break. With such a five-step break, the catcher will be made to feel that a quick throw to first will pick off the runner for the third out of the inning. However, he can't be given the luxury of sufficient time first to check the length of lead of the runner at third. For this reason, the runner at first doesn't move any farther up the line than he must to draw the throw from the catcher. This is crucial because the runner at third wants to get the best possible break. After all, the catcher is only throwing a distance of 90 feet, not the much longer 127 feet to second.

Obviously then, an excellent break is needed toward the plate. That break must begin just as soon as the catcher is seen pivoting toward first and cocking his arm for the throw there. If the catcher first tries to check the runner at third, he won't have enough time to get the runner at first. A throw to third will merely neutralize the play as all runners will return to their bases safely. The front runner must not allow himself to be so far down the line as to be in danger of being picked off.

The success of the play is based on three surprises. The first is the sudden break by the runner at first, which it is hoped will draw a throw from the catcher. The second comes as the front runner breaks for the plate as soon as the catcher commits himself to that throw. However, without the third surprise, the play will usually fail because a putout at first will end the inning before the run crosses the plate. Often, the first baseman won't even notice the front runner breaking. But whether he does or not, he will often go for the tag of the runner returning to first with a sweeping tag. But what he won't be aware of is the third surprise. The runner won't be there! Even though that runner will have stopped suddenly after his five-step fake break and will have begun what appeared to be a hurried return toward the bag, he will stop short of first and outside of the reach of the first baseman. He won't have to remain in a rundown very long before the charging front runner scores. Even if the first baseman takes one step toward the runner before deciding to throw home, it probably will be too late. If the first baseman is left-handed, his pivot to throw home will be more difficult.

For the defense to come out ahead, the first baseman must not hesitate in relaying the ball back to the plate. Even then, it should be a close play due to the good break of the runner at third. It is important that the back runner do a good acting job in pretending to want to return to first quickly to draw the catcher's throw without the latter having time to check the back runner.

★★

Drills and methods of instruction for Chapter 9 may be found on pages 174–79.

★★

10

Baserunning Drills

Practice does not make perfect! Practicing *proper techniques* makes perfect! And that is just what drills are—repetitions of a proper technique in an often simulated game atmosphere. With baserunning, those proper techniques and situations are the very same as those that have been emphasized throughout this book. The more closely the drills can be made to resemble actual ball-game situations, the better. They will prove to be nothing more than coverage of as many as possible of the baserunning techniques and situations encountered in a game.

It is often forgotten, too, that such drilling can be far more fun, educational, and interesting and just as physically demanding as doing sprints and other running exercises during preseason conditioning. This will also save time for work on other phases of the game.

The pattern of instruction in both strategy and technique usually follows a three-phase direction. It consists of lecture followed by demonstration followed by drill.

The lecture covers the role of the player, the importance of the topic, and a description of the strategy surrounding the execution of the drill. At the completion of the lecture the players should be anxiously awaiting the coach's explanation of the techniques involved. The instructional pattern then moves very naturally into the second phase, namely, demonstration. For the most part, the coach can often serve as demonstrator while lecturing to the group. After all, he knows better than anyone what techniques must be placed on exhibition in the demonstration. At this point, players must be strongly encouraged to ask any questions still existing in their minds. Mistakes and misconceptions seen during drills can be reduced drastically if players enter these drills with heads filled with confidence rather than with questions and doubts. All too often coaches rush into drills without adequate lecture or demonstration. Unfortunately, they usually pay for this impatience by finding themselves being repeatedly halted to re-explain one technique or another during a drill.

With proper presentation, however, the drill should represent the third and final phase of instruction. Manpower placement, logistics, and discipline are crucial to a well-orchestrated drill. The coach must place and move his players through a drill like any Hollywood director. Into how many lines do the players divide? Where do the lines start and where do the players go after completing their turns? What is expected of them while others are participating? When do players on defense get their chances? The coach must be ready to handle all these logistical questions quickly and efficiently.

Drills must be critiqued. This requires on-the-spot advice and correction as well as praise for achievement. Remember, practice will not improve a player's skills unless his techniques are correct. Otherwise, without on-the-spot critiquing, a player will only find himself becoming more firmly mired in bad habits despite his desire for the opposite.

While it is always nice to have the feel of a beautiful baseball diamond underfoot, it is true, nonetheless, that much can be accomplished indoors, especially during the preseason when the weather is often far from ideal. Besides eliminating the bad-weather factor, a classroom or gym-floor setting can also help to focus the players' attention on the words of the coach.

The arrangement of the following drills is in sequence with the chapter-by-chapter development of the entire book. Therefore, the first group of drills deals with the topics discussed in the early chapters. Those drills associated with the multiple-runner situations of Chapter 9 are near the end. The time to be spent on a drill or its number of repetitions is sometimes suggested, but such matters are best left to the coach. Such time and repetition decisions must be based on the importance of the drill to the team as well as the rapidity by which the players appear to be mastering the skills involved. For drills requiring some form or analysis, the necessary forms may be found in the Appendix. Many times, too, the baserunning practice will actually be more lecture than drill. This type of instruction involves the coach in talking to his players, sometimes using a blackboard, sometimes demonstrating, sometimes asking questions, and sometimes asking for comments and answers, but always in a serious mood and with the complete attention of the entire squad.

Besides the sequential arrangement of drills, each also bears the title of the corresponding chapter and pages where the involved technique or strategy is explained. Further, each drill is prefaced by a lesson objective.

What must be remembered is that the mastery of the techniques and strategies of aggressive baserunning will never become a reality without hard work, and that means plenty of practice. Each player and coach might do well to consider the words of an old grammar school rhyme as their motto regarding drills and their desire to improve. It goes like this: "Good, better, best, Never let it rest, 'Til the good is better, And the better best!"

CHAPTER 1. AGGRESSIVE BASERUNNING—THE MENTAL PERSPECTIVE

(Pages 1–3)

Lesson Objective: To instill a proper mental outlook regarding the team's plans for aggressiveness on the bases.

Drill or Method of Instruction: A complete explanation by the coach of the benefits to be gained and a description of the needed player qualities for this end to be achieved.

CHAPTER 2. RUNNING BY THE RULES

(Pages 5–10)

Lesson Objective: To acquaint the players with baseball rules pertaining to baserunning.

Drill or Method of Instruction: A give-and-take, question-and-answer discussion of baserunning rules with the coach using the twenty-four items of Chapter 2 as an outline.

CHAPTER 3. THE MECHANICS AND STRATEGY OF SLIDING

(Pages 11–14)

Lesson Objective: To ingrain in the players' minds the necessity for learning proper sliding techniques and the many uses of slides; to present some general reminders; and to describe some safeguards and sliding aids that can greatly reduce the chance of injury.

Drill or Method of Instruction: This introduction to sliding drills can be given indoors or outdoors. It could ever be given in a classroom prior to taking the field for actual sliding instruction and drill. A lecture by the coach should serve this purpose. Samples of sliding pads, sanitary socks, and even ankle or knee bandages should be available for inspection as their uses are discussed.

(Pages 14–33)

Lesson Objective: To teach the strategy, mechanics, and execution of as many as ten different slides.

Drill or Method of Instruction: For proper comprehension and learning, no more than one type of slide should ever be taught and drilled during any one practice session. Besides, sliding is baserunning and baserunning of one form or another should comprise a part of every practice. Therefore, there is plenty of time to cover as many of these slides as the coach desires over a period of a season, especially since a number of them are variations not frequently used.

While some may consider sliding pits as representative of the ideal situation, most teams must do without such luxuries. Realistically, then, an outdoor location might well be a lush, grassy area in the outfield or perhaps a wet grassy area following a rain. Indoors, a heavy plastic sheet can be placed on top of long wrestling mats with the extra plastic tucked under. Then, the players' pants as well as the plastic sheet are sprayed with silicone. This provides for a very fast but realistic slide. Another possibility is to spray water on the plastic sheet. It is wetter this way, but no silicone is needed. The simplest, however, is to use the gym floor. Players wear gym shoes and one or two pairs of old pants or sweatpants. Knee pads help. Indoors or outdoors, the bases used are most definitely loose and in no way fastened or spiked down.

Once the sliding area has been set up, the players begin with a two-way leadoff stance about 80 feet away from the base. They come flying, one at a time, with the coach standing near the slide area, making on-the-spot appraisals and perhaps keeping a checklist of needed improvements. At least five "perfect" slides should be required of each player. Those having difficulty are worked with longer, perhaps getting in ten or more slides in the practice session.

CHAPTER 4. WHAT EVERY BASERUNNER SHOULD KNOW

(Pages 35–36)

Lesson Objective: To acquaint players with some common-sense guidelines to follow when perched on any base or in a lead-off position on those bases; to familiarize the players with the team's signal system.

Drill or Method of Instruction: Best handled in a classroom, this instruction begins with a lecture that covers both general baserunning principles and the team's signal system. To test the players' understanding of the signals, the coach disguises the signals as he would at his third-base coaching position. He then asks the team to interpret those signs. He might wish to call on individual players or might even wish to have the players place their answers on paper as part of a written test. In one form or another, this kind of review and testing of the signals must be repeated from time to time until the coach is assured that the players understand them thoroughly.

(Page 37)

Lesson Objective: To remind players of certain common situations they will often encounter when advancing on the base path; to provide advice for handling these situations; to drill players in circling the bases efficiently.

Drill or Method of Instruction: Following a lecture on the principles to be mastered, the coach places eight runners on the base path, four on the bases and the other four at the midpoints between the bases. To begin, each player pretends that his left leg is in contact with a base. Actually, only four will have to pretend. All runners, upon a signal from the coach, will break as they would when trying to advance after a fly ball is caught in the outfield. Approaching the next base, however, the runners angle out, tag the base, and continue on.

Their objective is to catch up to and tag the next runner before they are tagged by the runner behind them. When a runner is eventually tagged, he quickly moves into the infield out of the way of the other runners still "alive." The drill continues until only four runners remain. This can be a great conditioner, especially if the coach is able to group runners of comparable speed so that the slower runners won't always be caught and eliminated quickly. Such slower runners will often be the ones most in need of this kind of drill. They will often gain confidence, too, when they find themselves able occasionally to overtake some runners.

(Pages 37–39)

Lesson Objective: To explain the strategy behind some common and some not-so-common multiple-runner situations not associated with any two particular bases.

Drill or Method of Instruction: In his lecture covering these points, the coach must be careful to avoid any confusion. It is best either to illustrate the situations on blackboard diagrams or have players "walk through" some of these happenings on an infield set up in the gym, if not outdoors. In addition, it is also best to restrict drilling these situations until they are met in sessions relating to Chapter 9, which concerns multiple-runner situations. At that time, players will learn that some of these plays will actually be planned and anticipated as a result of a special play or strategy.

CHAPTER 5. FROM THE DUGOUT TO FIRST

(Pages 41–43)

Lesson Objective: To familiarize the players with their baserunning responsibilities prior to hitting the ball.

Drill or Method of Instruction: A demonstrative, on-field lecture is utilized, covering baserunning responsibilities from the dugout, on-deck circle, and batters' box.

(Page 43)

Lesson Objective: To advise players on how to leave the batters' box under a variety of circumstances and on the use of proper footwork on a hit ball.

Drill or Method of Instruction: The coach verbally explains the strategy involved. Then, each player, in turn, mimics a good swing at the plate and sprints to first. Next, the players repeat the drill against live pitching. The coach watches for the occasional player whose footwork needs help and works with him more extensively.

(Pages 43–45)

Lesson Objective: To time the players' speeds from home to first.

Drill or Method of Instruction: Each player, in turn, attempts to bunt a pitched ball. As soon as the bat makes contact with the ball, even if the ball is fouled off, the batter takes off for first. The coach or timekeeper starts the stopwatch at this moment and, of course, stops the watch when the player touches first. The time is recorded and also announced to the player. The coach makes certain that the batter makes contact with the ball while in the batters' box and also corrects any runner who tags the bag improperly or who fails to run through the bag. This is a good drill to repeat several times over the course of the season. Players will usually be quite intent on trying to lower their times.

(Pages 43–47)

Lesson Objective: To explain the many components that go into a well-performed sprint from home to first; to teach techniques that will maximize each player's speed in this sprint; to involve players in an analysis of their teammates' running styles to first base; to provide each player with a 23-point checklist of his own running characteristics.

Drill or Method of Instruction: To begin, the coach explains and demonstrates the many thoughts and techniques that comprise the run from home to first. Then, nine stations are set up along the first baseline, manned by one to two players at each station depending on the size of the roster. Actually, these players position themselves in foul territory since batters will be swinging at a pitched ball. However, for safety purposes a rag or tennis or rubber ball is used since a number of players will be standing relatively close to the batter along the baseline. A batting order is established and a couple of players assigned to pitch, catch, and retrieve the hit ball.

Next, each station is provided with a pencil and copy of an analysis sheet found on page 182 in the Appendix. Because the sheet is designed to be used for just two players, the names of the first two hitters are penciled in at the top of the sheet. When the first batter hits the ball, he sprints to first as he would for any ground ball in a game. He does this even if the ball is something other than an infield grounder. Besides, no first baseman is used anyway. The player or players at each of the nine stations watch for the techniques mentioned in the checklist and mark it accordingly. After the second batter has run his sprint to first, all checklists are collected. Later, the information will be compiled into one neat summary sheet for each player.

At this point, the player or players at station A (closest to home) come in to hit, those at station B move to station A, and so on down the line. The last two hitters are then assigned to station I near first base. New checklists are provided for each pair of hitters. This procedure continues until all players have hit and been analyzed. The coach sees to it that those in the field get their chances, too. It is in the coach's spare time, not on the field, that the data from the checklists is reorganized and compiled. At the next practice, the coach may distribute a team summary sheet. Although he may make some general remarks about the team's performance as a whole, he may also wish to discuss individual performances on a one-to-one basis. The next time that the players run to first in drills intended to maximize their speeds, both player and coach will know exactly what weaknesses to watch for and on which to work. At that time, no positioning of players at stations will be necessary unless the coach wishes to measure improvement through another complete analysis after some time has passed.

(Pages 43–45)

Lesson Objective: To increase the force and length of the stride.

Drill or Method of Instruction: Known in track circles as the Knee Lift or High Knee Drill, this involves first running in place with emphasis on a maximum knee lift. These lifts should be powerful yet produced with minimal tension. Relaxation is the key. Next, under the coach's direction, the players run 100 feet utilizing this exaggerated high-knee movement. The higher the knee, the more forceful will be the leg's contact with the ground when it hits down. Three to four such runs should be executed. In time, this practice movement will produce more forceful steps and a lengthened stride.

Another track drill utilized by sprinters has the runner straightening his lower leg upon completion of his knee lift. At this point the lower leg is forcefully flung downward and then backward as the body moves forward as a result. While not used as part of the natural running style, this exaggerated movement, which some compare to that of a running ostrich, will eventually produce a lengthened and more forceful stride. Again, three to four such 100-foot runs should suffice during a practice session.

(Page 46)

Lesson Objective: To acquaint the players with the role of the first-base coach and to teach just what the coach can and cannot do for the batter-runner.

Drill or Method of Instruction: The logic involved in the communication between the batter-runner and the first-base coach is best handled through an explanation by the coach in a lecture format. A make-believe first-base line and coach's box will help, too, if the discussion is held indoors.

(Pages 47–48)

Lesson Objective: To provide practice in the proper and most efficient technique for rounding the base at first.

Drill or Method of Instruction: Each player, in turn, takes a phantom swing at the plate, getting a make-believe base hit to the field of his choice, which he names. With the prior "rounding" technique having been explained by the coach prior to the drill, the players round first aggressively, stop, and then follow the make-believe throw back into the infield. Besides correcting errors, the coach should take note of those players who have difficulties and their respective problems. This list will help when the drill is repeated in the future. In this way, the coach can note any improvement, too.

(Pages 48–50)

Lesson Objective: To provide situations through which batter-runners will receive experience in making decisions after aggressively rounding the bag at first, the decision being between that of stretching the hit into two bases or returning to first.

Drill or Method of Instruction: The coach first lectures the team on situations that favor an attempt at two bases. Then, with a complete defense on the field, the runners line up at home plate where the coach fungoes hits of various kinds for the runners. Upon rounding first, the runner must decide whether or not the circumstances warrant a try for two bases. This drill also provides practice in sliding, since most of the attempts at two bases will result in a close play necessitating a slide.

CHAPTER 6. MOVING FROM FIRST BASE TO SECOND

(Pages 51–52)

Lesson Objective: To produce within each player a sense of awareness regarding his newfound status as a runner at first base.

Drill or Method of Instruction: Indoors or outdoors, the coach, while mimicking a runner, toes first base while lecturing the players on just what should be going through their minds at this point.

(Page 53)

Lesson Objective: To advise players of the dos and don'ts in the art of moving off the bag.

Drill or Method of Instruction: Indoors or outdoors, the coach will again mimic the runner as he demonstrates proper techniques. Then he will watch as each player in turn performs this short and simple, yet important movement in front of him.

(Pages 53–57)

Lesson Objective: To familiarize the players with the proper techniques and factors governing the use, angle, and length of the two-way leadoff, the one-way leadoff, the secondary lead, and the fake steal.

Drill or Method of Instruction: The coach lectures the players on the proper techniques involved while the entire squad is spread out in front of him in a squadron-type lineup with ample room between players. Upon command, the whole squad, pretending to be in contact with the base, is first asked to move off the bag into a two-way leadoff stance and then, upon signal, to assume a secondary lead. After several repetitions, the one-way lead and the fake steal are handled similarly. In addition, or in place of this procedure, the coach may wish to put each player through these paces in a one-on-one set-up. This drill can be performed equally well indoors or outdoors.

(Pages 57–65)

Lesson Objective: To instruct players in the proper methods of returning to first base upon a pickoff attempt.

Drill or Method of Instruction: After a lecture and demonstration by the coach, the players are drilled in groups of five. The five players line up, one behind the other, approximately three to four strides off the first-base line. Only the first man in line will be able actually to use the base. The others will approximate the location of the base by drawing one with their spikes. The coach will ask the group to return to the bag using each of the three acceptable methods. The choice of return used by a player in a game will often be dictated by the length of leadoff. Therefore, depending on whether he is asked in this drill to return on the left foot, right foot, or by way of a dive, the player will have to adjust his leadoff length. The coach may prefer to watch each player individually rather than in groups. In addition, the drill can easily be performed indoors, although knee pads are recommended for the diving returns on a hard surface.

(Pages 53–65)

Lesson Objective: To make players aware of their own quickness, the length of leadoff best for them, and the various methods for returning to the bag.

Drill or Method of Instruction: This drill utilizes a pitcher and catcher. Each player, in turn, practices returning to the bag at first as the pitcher throws over and later as the catcher snaps a pickoff throw to the first baseman. For the pickoff throws by the pitcher, the coach first asks players to assume a two-way leadoff. Then, for a second throw-over, the runners are asked to assume a one-way leadoff. Next, for the pickoff throws by the catcher, the runners first go into ordinary secondary leads before returning quickly, and finally, they perform another quick return following a fake steal. In every case, the runners wear helmets.

The coach may utilize the option of either watching each player go through one of these types of return before moving on to the next type or watching one player perform all four types of returns before going on to the next player. Players finding themselves picked off will go through the same type of return again, this time shortening the lead or making any other necessary correction. Players able to return very easily will also repeat the return, this time increasing the lead. The coach may ask a player to continue increasing his lead until finally he is picked off. In this way the runner can learn just how great a leadoff he is capable of taking—for *that* pitcher and catcher!

(Pages 53–56, 66)

Lesson Objective: To teach the proper baserunning response to a sacrifice bunt, especially in regard to the timing of the secondary lead as compared to the non-bunt situation.

Drill or Method of Instruction: After instruction, each player, in turn, responds accordingly in his secondary lead as a batting-practice hitter swings or bunts at the ball as instructed by the coach, who is standing near the batter. If the ball is missed, the catcher snaps a quick throw to the first baseman. Runners attempt to continue to third on bunts fielded by the third baseman. Several rounds are used.

(Page 66)

Lesson Objective: To produce a proper sense of awareness in the mind of the baserunner when he sees a line drive or fly ball come off the bat of the hitter with less than two outs.

Drill or Method of Instruction: First, the coach lectures on the advisibility of attempting to tag up and possibly advance on certain types of fly balls. One at a time, players then assume a two-way lead and then a secondary lead as the coach fungoes fly balls. He will vary the depth and location of the fly balls in an attempt to make the base runner think and respond prudently. A complete set of defensive players is used while the rest of the team acts as runners. Another drill used to sharpen players' reactions to line drives is described below.

(Pages 67–68)

Lesson Objective: To inform players of the correct responses to ground balls hit to various infield positions with different numbers of outs.

Drill or Method of Instruction: The coach spends time carefully lecturing on the four main ground-ball situations that may be encountered. Because most of these situations will result in either rounding the bag, going into a pop-up slide, or upsetting a pivot man, the coach must insist upon good sliding techniques. As a consequence, the baserunner not only gains experience reacting to ground balls, but also sharpens his sliding skills as well under a realistic ball-game situation.

To begin the drill, the coach places a runner at first and calls out the number of outs before fungoing a ground ball to an infielder. A runner also starts out from home plate. The coach may wish the runner at home to fungo the ground ball himself.

The runners to be used at first are lined up along the foul area near first base. Several rounds constitute the drill. The defense players situated in the infield must be given their chances to run, too.

(Pages 68–69)

Lesson Objective: To train players to respond correctly when reacting to a base hit to the outfield, but also including the line drive snared by an infielder; to drill players in making the decision either to stop at second or continue on to third; to teach players when to make this decision themselves and when help might be coming from the third-base coach.

Drill or Method of Instruction: Following the coach's lecture on the strategy and execution of this play, a complete defense is placed on the field. The remaining players take turns in one of two lines, one line supplying runners at first while the other supplies hitters to bat base-hit fungoes to the outfielders. The coach stands in the third-base coaching box signaling the runner whenever the play is behind him. Runners get practice in both lines, and defensive players eventually get their chances to run, too.

(Pages 69–70)

Lesson Objective: To teach players the strategy of the hit-and-run play.

Drill or Method of Instruction: The coach first explains the techniques and strategy of the hit-and-run play, being sure to point out the various responsibilities required of the batter and the runner at first. Then, after placing a complete defense on the field, he splits the remaining squad members into two lines. One line represents hitters who are stationed near home plate. The other line represents the runners who stand in foul territory near first base.

A hitter then steps to the plate while a runner at first assumes his leadoff. As a live pitch is delivered, the runner breaks for second and, shortly after, takes his look in toward the plate. The batter, of course, tries to make contact and hit the ball on the ground toward right field. If the ball isn't hit, the entire play is killed, a new runner taking over to save time. Because more pitches will be received by the catcher than hit, the catcher is instructed not to throw down since his arm would soon be hanging.

For each ball hit, the batter, runner, and defense must react even if the ball is not ideally hit into right field or behind the runner. Sliding is required when necessary. Whenever the play is behind the runner, arm signals are given to the runner by the coach from his coaching position at third base. As long as the ball is hit at all, the play is completed. Then, the bases are vacated with the participants returning to the end of the opposite line. After sufficient opportunities to hit and run, places are exchanged with the defensive players to give them opportunities to execute the play.

(Pages 70–71, 101–103)

Lesson Objective: To instill a healthy and positive mental outlook toward base stealing; to instruct players in some general principles governing the study of pitchers' moves both to home and to first; to study the anatomy of a steal by examining a time line of this classic play.

Drill or Method of Instruction: The instruction is best given indoors since attention is a must and because a paper will be distributed and studied along with a "base stealing time line" which is best drawn on a blackboard. Like good baserunning in general, but now with base stealing in particular, an aggressive, determined, and enthusiastic attitude must be fostered within the players by the coach. They must be made to want that successful steal very badly. Most important, the point must be made that base stealing requires more than speed alone if success is to be realized on a frequent basis. Otherwise, the fast runner will sit back thinking that he possesses the only necessary credential to successful base stealing. Furthermore, the runner with average speed must be made to understand that with study and practice much can be accomplished. He can become a fine base stealer through "smarts" and quickness, if not outright speed.

Once these points have been covered, some general principles related to the study of a pitcher's moves are mentioned before any closer study is made of the mechanics of the pitcher's form. This closer scrutiny will be handled in later sessions. For this session, the next step is to lecture around the time-line anatomy of a steal which may be found on page 103. This time line should either be drawn on the blackboard or mimeographed and distributed at the meeting. Either way, all its fine points are studied and discussed in a give-and-take format in which the players are encouraged to participate and say whatever comes to mind.

(Pages 71–100)

Lesson Objective: To discuss the charting of the types of pickoff moves to both first and second made by an opposing pitcher; to examine both a blank and completed chart of this move; and to demonstrate the value of such charting to a team's baserunning plan.

Drill or Method of Instruction: The scouting form for pitchers' moves to first and second is distributed to the players in a classroom. The method of charting is explained by the coach. He also mimics the pitchers' various moves as he goes along to facilitate the explanation. After discussing the importance and relevance of keeping such a form, the coach then distributes a completed form, one that he perhaps kept himself while watching a game in person or on television. He and the players then study the completed form to determine what baserunning knowledge might be learned. For practice, the players should be encouraged to chart a pitcher's moves using the blank form given them. This could be done at home or at a live game. From this point on, players should be made to understand that any one of them might be called upon during a game to handle this charting.

(Pages 71–84)

Lesson Objective: To acquaint the players with the many pickoff characteristics that a right-handed pitcher may display as opposed to his pitching motion; to teach players to analyze the motions of pitchers in their search for these characteristics.

Drill or Method of Instruction: Either indoors or outdoors, the coach uses a player or himself to demonstrate the 10 characteristics that may differentiate a pitcher's pickoff move to first from his throw to the plate. Since the coach may be giving the demonstration himself, he can make each characteristic as obvious as he likes, although the players must be warned that some of these characteristics may well be negligible or even nonexistent with many pitchers. Usually, however, at least one and sometimes more of these telltale traits will be seen with every right-handed pitcher.

Upon completion of the lecture and demonstration, a

charting sheet for right-handed pitchers is distributed to each team member. This chart may be found on page 190 of the Appendix. The names of the team's right-handed pitchers are then written at the top along with the charter's name. Next, the coach will ask one right-handed pitcher at a time to alternate throws to home and to first for a 5-minute period. With the exception of the pitcher, catcher, and first baseman, the other team members station themselves in the baseline between first and second. This will produce a view of the pitcher similar to the one viewed by a runner at first. Each player fills in a "yes" or "no" for each of the seven body characteristics indicated. "Yes" indicates a characteristic that most definitely stands out and which could be used by a runner to gain an advantage on his break to second. "No" indicates that a particular trait is either nonexistent or fails to manifest itself sufficiently to warrant a player's study of that trait in the pitcher. When all seven body traits have been given a "yes" or "no," the player completes his analysis by circling the "yes" (assuming he has indicated two or more) that he feels is the pitcher's most telltale motion characteristic.

Then, before a new right-handed pitcher goes to the mound, the coach asks for the team's findings. A consensus of opinion should not be expected in most cases. However, the pitcher is then asked to throw a couple more pitches and pickoffs so that all participants can zero in on that characteristic mentioned most often. Of course, the catchers and first basemen should also alternate so that they, too, can get a chance to chart. The drill concludes when all of the right-handed pitchers have been given their 5 or 6 minutes of pitching. This drill can be a great help to the pitchers, too, especially when they may learn surprisingly that their pitch or pickoff intentions can be readily determined by a runner.

That evening, the coach may wish to tabulate the team's findings for each pitcher and to present those findings to each pitcher at the next practice. It would be good, too, for the coach to keep a copy of these findings so he can check periodically on the improvement of his pitchers' motions in the future. This chart could also be kept during actual games.

(Pages 84–100)

Lesson Objective: To acquaint the players with 8 pickoff characteristics that a left-handed pitcher may display as opposed to his motion when he throws home; to teach players to analyze the motions of left-handed pitchers in their search for these characteristics.

Drill or Method of Instruction: The coach may use a player or himself either indoors or outdoors to point out the characteristics in a left-handed pitcher's motion that may differ when he attempts a pickoff as opposed to throwing home. Again, after lecturing the players, the coach distributes a form for analyzing the motions of the left-handers on the club. This form may be found in the Appendix on page 192. The left-handed pitchers on the club will each get about 5 minutes apiece to throw from the mound, alternating pitches with pickoffs. A catcher and first baseman will assume their positions while the remainder of the team will place themselves in positions similar to that of a runner at first. In the absence of more than one or two left-handed pitchers on the club, the coach may ask a couple of other left-handed players to pretend they are pitchers just to give the others more practice in viewing these various characteristics.

With an analysis form in the hands of each player, the coach reviews the procedure with the players. Directions are also given on the form. Each left-handed pitcher's form is discussed when he finishes his pitching and when all of the players have seen sufficient pitches and pickoffs to complete their analyses. This can be a great help to the pitcher, too, in his desire to improve his own pickoff motion. Everything else in this drill follows the same format as in the previous drill. Remember, too, that this form could also be kept during a game in scouting the moves of the opposing pitcher.

(Pages 104–110)

Lesson Objective: To demonstrate and drill two acceptable methods of breaking for second as the pitcher begins his move to the plate. These two methods are also the most popular.

Drill or Method of Instruction: The techniques of both methods are first explained and demonstrated in the gym by the coach. He then critiques these breaks as his players line up and one at a time perform at least five of each type. Then, each player is timed twice, utilizing each type of break for a 40-foot sprint, in an attempt to determine if a player is finding better success with one method than the other. If so, he is encouraged to stay with that method. Of course, because the times will be so close over that short distance, it is extremely important that the same exact starting point be used for all the timings.

(Pages 71–101, 104–111)

Lesson Objective: To provide players with practice in reading the moves of pitchers and in getting a good break on a steal attempt.

Drill or Method of Instruction: Indoors, a pitcher throws from the stretch while players lead off and break, one at a time, from a position similar to that of a runner at first. The coach may even wish to set up two pitchers throwing from the stretch, one left-hander and one right-hander. Then, when the runner completes his break against one pitcher, he proceeds to the end of the other line.

(Pages 71–101, 104–111)

Lesson Objective: To practice sprinting and breaking at the same time, utilizing multiple runners for each pitch.

Drill or Method of Instruction: Three players at a time line up one behind the other at first base and assume their leadoffs. Of course, only the front man is in proper position on the baseline, but all three are in good position to see the pitcher and his moves. Performed indoors or outdoors, this drill finds the coach assuming the position of the pitcher. No catcher or first baseman is used. Sometimes the coach pretends to go home with his make-believe pitch, while at other times he will pretend to throw to first. The players try to read his moves accordingly. If he does go home, the players not only break toward second, but continue their sprint for a full 90 feet. If conditions permit, the steal might be concluded with a slide if the coach desires. The coach should also use a pitcher who throws with the opposite arm to take his place halfway through the drill in order to provide practice against both lefties and righties.

(Pages 71–101, 104–111)

Lesson Objective: To provide a complete and more realistic setting in the drilling of steal attempts.

Drill or Method of Instruction: As each player completes his turn in batting practice, he assumes the position of a runner at first. A complete infield is on the field. The pitcher then throws the first several pitches to the next hitter from the set position, throwing over to first as necessary to keep the runner close to the bag. The runner is under instructions to steal on a pitch of his choosing. When the steal does occur, the catcher throws to second as the steal attempt is completed with a slide. At that point, the pitcher may resume batting-practice pitching from any position he likes until the next batter completes his turn and becomes the next runner at first.

(Pages 104–11)

Lesson Objective: To familiarize the players with four special kinds of breaks and the circumstances under which they can be best utilized.

Drill or Method of Instruction: First, the advantages, strategy, and techniques of these four special breaks are pointed out and demonstrated by the coach either indoors or outdoors. Then, going through one special break at a time, team members in rotation are given the chance to execute each of them. Those having any difficulty are asked to repeat them until the coach is satisfied. The coach may wish to get in some additional sliding practice by having the players complete their breaks and run with a slide of one type or another. All the while, the coach is standing close by, scrutinizing both the breaks and the slides.

(Pages 111–112)

Lesson Objective: To provide advice and experience regarding the unenviable position of being caught in a rundown.

Drill or Method of Instruction: Performed indoors or outdoors, this drill utilizes a complete infield along with a runner at first. The runner, for the purpose of this drill, allows himself to be picked off at first by the pickoff throw of the pitcher. Instead of trying to return to the bag, he opts for his chances in a rundown. The advantages are most definitely with the defense, but the advice given the players prior to the start of this drill are put into practice.

The coach stands close by to critique both the defense and the runner. To get more players into the drill, the coach may prefer to forego the normal diamond setup and instead simulate three baselines parallel to each other. Two defensive players are placed at each base, that is, a total of four for each base path. The rundown begins with the ball in the hands of one of the defensive players, supposedly the first baseman who has just taken the pickoff throw and has caught the runner flat-footed. The runner begins his part of the drill about three strides from this fielder. Three of these rundowns may be going on simultaneously. While the defense players try to get their man in just one throw or two at the very most, the runners have some other ideas as they try their best to escape the putout.

CHAPTER 7. ADVANCING FROM SECOND BASE TO THIRD

(Pages 113–17)

Lesson Objective: To familiarize the players with proper techniques regarding the runner's station at second base, his lead-off there, his base-stealing possibilities, and some special steal plays he may utilize.

Drill or Method of Instruction: To teach these techniques indoors on a make-believe, cut-down infield could prove very deceiving with respect to leadoffs, steals, and pickoffs. Outdoors then, the coach, after lecturing the players on these techniques, works with one player at a time. He checks each player's leadoff angle, manner of leading off, length of lead, and ability to relay a catcher's signals back to the batter. Then, with a shortstop and second baseman jockeying back and forth to keep the runner close and with a pitcher on the mound, the coach calls out advice from the third-base coaching box and scrutinizes the runner's reactions. A catcher is used to flash some obvious signals and to receive pitches, too. In fact, an entire defense is placed on the field. The pitcher may attempt a pickoff whenever he wishes.

This drill is incorporated with an ongoing batting practice on the same diamond. Besides the catcher's giving signals, the pitcher throws all pitches from the stretch, trying to keep the runner close. This will provide a more realistic setting for the runner but will also result in a slower batting practice. Both conventional and special steals of third will be discussed and practiced at this time, too. However, a simple signal system will be used to provide the needed element of surprise for the defense. The runner's steal and slide into third will conclude that player's baserunning practice.

(Page 117)

Lesson Objective: To teach and practice the strategies and techniques of the sacrifice bunt and the bunt-and-steal play.

Drill or Method of Instruction: Because these plays involve the bunt, the coach can work on both during the same session. He begins with an explanation of the strategies and mechanics of the two plays, choreographing the runner's movements on a blackboard or on the diamond itself. After a complete infield is in position, the remaining team members are divided into runners and bunters, the players alternating lines after each performance. The coach may wish to practice the two plays separately, but it might be more interesting to keep the defense guessing and keep the offense thinking by mixing the plays. This is done through a simple signal system to inform each bunter and runner of what play is on.

(Pages 117–19)

Lesson Objective: To inject prudent guidelines for running, not running, or delaying on ground balls and hits.

Drill or Method of Instruction: First, the numerous possibilities that could result when a ground ball is hit, especially in the direction of third or short, are discussed. For each possibility, a general guideline is presented. The consequences of a hit are also mentioned. Next, a complete defense is positioned on the field while the remaining team players are split into two groups and utilized as either runners at second base or hitters at the plate. However, for quickness of drill and to provide sufficient variation, the coach fungoes the ground balls and hits. The runners and hitters alternate lines and eventually move to the field to get practice there, too. The hitters start out from the batters' box on the right side. When the play is completed, all runners vacate their bases. On throws to the plate following hits to the outfield, cuts should be encouraged and called out by the catcher. Hitters are placed on their own in attempting to take an extra base on a base hit followed by a throw to the plate.

(Pages 119–20)

Lesson Objective: To gain practice in making prudent decisions following fly balls when positioned at second base.

Drill or Method of Instruction: The drill begins with a lecture, perhaps indoors in a room with a blackboard. Fly balls that stand any chance of being caught are subdivided into four types with guidelines given for dealing with each type. The coach then moves outdoors with the team and sets up a complete defense on the field. The others take turns running at second base and running from home. Runners are needed at the plate since the coach, hitting fungoes of varying depths, will be sure to hit some that won't be caught. After each play the bases are vacated, and the previous batter moves to second base while a new batter moves to the plate. The hitter starts out from the right-handed batters' box as the fungo is hit. Even with easily caught flies, the batter can still work on several aspects of his run to first and his turn to second. Later, of course, the defensive players will be given a chance to run as former runners take their places in the field.

CHAPTER 8. THE LAST 90 FEET TO THE PLATE

(Pages 121–25)

Lesson Objective: To teach proper leadoff technique at third base; to make players aware of the importance of their state of awareness at that base.

Drill or Method of Instruction: Indoors or outdoors, the coach lectures the players on leadoff techniques at third base. He also makes them aware of the several unexpected chances to score. For that reason, he must emphasize the importance of awareness and alertness. Next, each player, in turn, is observed in his leadoff technique, but not before the coach has fully explained and demonstrated the technique. Once the coach is satisfied that the players understand these directions, the drill can take on an added dimension. A pitcher, catcher, and third baseman are positioned. One at a time, team members take their positions as runners at third. With a runner in position, the pitcher prepares to pitch from the stretch. He may attempt a pickoff if he desires. Otherwise, he pitches while the runner goes through his right-left-right walking lead. Then, if the coach with either a verbal call, a clap of the hands, or a whistle communicates that the pitch has been hit on the ground, the runner sprints home. If nothing is heard, the runner quickly returns to the base as if the pitch wasn't hit. The catcher may elect to attempt a pickoff at third after the pitch.

(Pages 125–26)

Lesson Objective: To explain the strategy of the tag-up at third on fly balls; to demonstrate the technique involved; to drill the players on the execution of this technique.

Drill or Method of Instruction: After the technique and strategy have been explained by the coach, a complete defense is positioned on the field. Then, the remaining team members line up in foul territory near third base to take their turn tagging up on flies fungoed by the coach. To avoid injury, the coach may elect either to refrain from sliding or to ask the catcher not to block the plate. Of course, helmets are always worn.

(Pages 125–26)

Lesson Objective: To drill player responses to ground balls and fly balls when leading off third base.

Drill or Method of Instruction: Incorporated into batting practice, this drill uses several players stationed in foul territory near third base along with a complete defense in the field. One of these runners assumes his lead at third and then reacts as he would in a game to the first ground ball or fly ball hit by the batting-practice hitter. With the completion of the play, a new runner moves in. In every case, the defense is instructed to make a play for the runner who is trying to score.

(Pages 126–27)

Lesson Objective: To explain the techniques involved in the steal of home and to drill the timing of the break.

Drill or Method of Instruction: After the coach lectures the team on the responsibilities of the runner and batter, he next emphasizes the importance of the big lead and quick jump. To point out just how great a lead is needed for the play to be successful, he may wish to do the following.

With a pitcher and catcher in position, each player, in turn, attempts to steal home without the use of a slide or a leadoff. In other words, he is in contact with third base when he makes his break. Of course, the ball will surely beat him to the plate by quite a distance. However, by noting where he was in the baseline when the ball reached the catcher, the runner will learn the length of leadoff needed for him to succeed. That leadoff will be approximately equal to the distance between home plate and the position of the runner when the ball reaches the catcher. Once that distance has been determined in the mind of each player, the drill can be repeated. This time, the runner will be allowed the luxury of a leadoff. He probably won't be timid either, since he will know how far down the line he must be when he makes his break. This time the steal will conclude with a slide, but the catcher should be reminded that it will be his teammates coming down the line and not the opposition. Team members should also take turns at bat to make the play more realistic and to provide opportunities to work on their responsibilities while batting. Both offensive players wear helmets.

(Pages 127–28)

Lesson Objective: To teach the strategy and mechanics of both types of squeeze plays; to provide drill in their execution.

Drill or Method of Instruction: Once the coach's lecture on the squeeze plays is completed, he places a complete defense on the field. The remaining players are used as runners and batters. A special signal system, perhaps an oral system using multiple numbers, is arranged for the offensive players. In this way, the coach can let each batter and runner combination know what play is on. To keep the defense honest, sometimes no play will be given, and the batter will be free to take a full cut. In fact, the coach might even like to incorporate a signal for a straight steal of home. Again, helmets are a must and so is sliding. The runners and batters alternate lines as they complete their turns. Later, they will exchange roles with the defensive players.

(Pages 128–29)

Lesson Objective: To explain the strategy of a special delayed steal play; to provide drill in its execution.

Drill or Method of Instruction: After an explanation of the play, the coach positions a complete infield and divides the rest of the team into batters and runners at third. As the pitcher delivers the pitch, the batter reacts to it as he would to a walk. The play continues with the batter-runner continuing with a break for second followed by the runner at third breaking for the plate. Upon completion of a play, the involved runners go to the rear of the opposite line of players to gain practice at both ends of the play. If desired, this play could be incorporated into a batting practice. The coach merely assigns a different runner to third base as each batter is completing his batting practice. Then, after a final pitch which the batter intentionally takes, the batter trots down to first and then breaks for second. This allows each player to practice the play twice, once as a batter and once as a runner at third.

CHAPTER 9. MULTIPLE-RUNNER SITUATIONS AND STRATEGIES

(Pages 132–35)

Lesson Objective: To prepare runners to respond properly to any of five possible plays that may be called with runners at first and second.

Drill or Method of Instruction: The coach begins by grouping the players together on the infield grass as he explains the strategies of the sacrifice bunt, double steal, double-steal–fake-bunt variation, double-steal–fake-bunt and slash-hit variation, and the double-steal–pickoff-at-first variation. He may not wish to include all five plays in his playbook. Using three players as his two runners and hitter, he walks them through each play that he does wish to include. Because the players have already been instructed and drilled in the techniques of bunting and stealing, the strategy explanation becomes all-important.

To drill, the coach places a complete defense on the field. He then meets with the remainder of the team to set up a simple, oral signal system (perhaps utilizing a number code) to disguise the various plays. The defense must be kept guessing. One signal is also reserved for the batter to take a full cut. These players will then take turns as runners and batter. Next, the coach signals the three participants. The pitcher delivers and the offense executes. The coach critiques both offensive and defensive performances and answers questions before clearing the bases for three new participants. When the nine defensive players are called in for their turns, a modified signal system is put into effect to keep the defense honest. Some coaches may prefer to drill these plays separately, but remember that in a game situation the offense must be able to respond correctly in a moment's notice to any of these plays when signaled by the coach. In this way, the players must think in the execution of this drill rather than responding like robots. This kind of multiple drill prepares them for any stunting that the coach may call for with runners at first and second.

(Pages 135–37)

Lesson Objective: To prepare runners stationed at second and third to react properly to all situations encountered there, including, among others, the single- and double-squeeze plays along with the special pickoff-at-second steal.

Drill or Method of Instruction: As in the previous section, the coach begins by first lecturing the players on proper techniques and strategies for the possible situations they will encounter at second and third. This can be done on the infield grass. He also carefully explains the special plays and will walk through each of them using two players and a batter to demonstrate. Again, a special signal system must be devised for those players taking turns as hitters and runners. The defense placed on the field must be kept guessing to be fair to the offense. A signal to hit away must also be included, thus requiring the need for outfielders. On a hit ball, the coach, standing near third, advises the runners on tagging on fly balls and on trying to score on ground balls and hits. When the defense is given its chance to practice these offensive skills, the signal system is changed again. The drill continues until the coach is relatively assured that each player knows how to react to these several situations and special plays. Of course, time will not allow every player to take on every possible role in every play. Hopefully, though, each player's participation complemented by the viewing of his teammates in action will sufficiently prepare him for any situation he may encounter.

(Pages 137–39)

Lesson Objective: To prepare players for the proper execution of the safety- and suicide-squeeze plays as well as the double-advancement play with runners at first and third.

Drill or Method of Instruction: To begin, the coach discusses the two types of squeeze plays and their strategic differences. In addition, he mentions some general reminders for the runner at third in all first and third situations. While the double advancement play rarely presents itself, this is an excellent time to explain its workings and to give the players a chance to get the feel of it. It is rarely seen, but the well-prepared and aggressive teams will always jump on an opportunity to use it. Again, all of these plays are walked through while the team is seated on the infield grass or in the dugout.

As with most multiple-runner drills, all three plays are drilled simultaneously to keep both the offense and defense thinking rather than just reacting from memory to one play. A complete infield is placed on the field although no outfield is necessary. A signal system is established to let each batter and set of runners know which variety of squeeze play is coming. Of course, with the safety squeeze most pitches out of the strike zone will be taken. Unless the catcher attempts a pickoff following the pitch, he is instructed to respond automatically by lofting a foul pop-up behind first base. The runners then go into their special double-advancement play. With a bunt always expected, the coach must make certain that the third baseman doesn't cheat by charging before the batter actually begins telegraphing his intentions. With each play, corrections and suggestions are made, but the coach must never forget to praise the well-executed play. Nor must the defense be forgotten. They deserve praise, too, when they respond well. And like the offense, the defensive players will be chomping at the bit to get their chances to run these plays against another group of infielders. The coach must remember to give them their chances, too.

(Pages 140–43)

Lesson Objective: To prepare runners at first and third as well as the batter to execute the hit-and run, fake double steal, regular double steal, and delayed double steal.

Drill or Method of Instruction: The coach first describes the techniques and strategies of these plays to the team. Then, with the team seated on the infield grass, a couple of players are asked to walk through the plays as they are explained and questions are answered. This time an outfield will be needed along with an infield for the hit-and-run play. To begin, the offensive players are divided into three groups to be used as batters, runners at first, and runners at third. As the players take their places, they receive a signal from the coach. Again, it's a simple signal system constructed to keep the defense guessing and the offense thinking. Only the offense must know what kind of play is coming. The pitcher delivers, the offense executes, the defense responds, the coach critiques, the bases are cleared, and new participants take their places. While the coach may decide to work on some or all of these plays individually, he should eventually advance to this drill encompassing all of them. The players must be made to realize that in a game they might receive a signal for any one of these plays. Of course, the coach may also find it wise to limit some of these plays, concentrating on certain ones while discarding others.

(Pages 143–46)

Lesson Objective: To teach players the techniques and strategies involved in as many as four walkoff or runoff plays for use with runners at first and third. This includes the intentional-pickoff double steal, which could well be considered a form of runoff.

Drill or Method of Instruction: Note that most teams will prefer to be selective here and limit these special plays to just one or two. The more plays that can be thrown at the defense, the better, but this holds only if the offense can correctly execute them. Even major-league teams limit them to near zero because the opposing teams' defenses are so strong that such plays rarely work. On the other hand, while such plays hold a much greater chance of success with amateur teams, time becomes an important factor. Most teams just lack sufficient time to drill and become proficient in all of them. They need time for other phases of the game. Because timing is so very important with these plays, those that are to be included in a team's playbook must be practiced individually. Only after they have been mastered on this kind of individual basis can they be practiced collectively.

When that time comes, drills similar to those already described for other multiple-runner situations can be utilized. However, to drill just one of these plays, only an infield is needed along with two runners. No batter or outfield is needed. After being instructed in the mechanics of the play, the offensive players in groups of two rotate in and out as runners, getting in practice at both bases. Only when the coach is satisfied with the performance of one play should he go on to another. The offensive players shouldn't get discouraged when a play fails, especially late in the practice session when they might feel that they should have the play down well. Perhaps they do, but by this time, the defense has also learned how best to respond and defend. Keep in mind, though, that when such plays are attempted in games, they will often succeed due to a defense that is totally surprised by the aggressiveness and daring demonstrated.

(Pages 137–46)

Lesson Objective: To review all situations and plays in the team's playbook for the first and third situation.

Drill or Method of Instruction: With a complete defense on the field and an offensive signal system arranged, the offense is divided into three groups. Each group of three is used as runners at first and third and the hitter at the plate. With a group in position, they are given a signal, execute, receive a critique, and then clear the bases for the next group. The individual members of each trio rotate roles each time they perform. The offensive players not being used at a given moment station themselves in foul territory far beyond first and third base and away from home plate. This way, there is less chance of anyone being hit by a stray throw or being a cause of distraction.

Besides the signals for various bunt and hit-and run plays, one should also be included to give the batter a chance to swing away without either of the runners moving until the ball is hit. This is a very difficult drill for the runners since it requires total recall of all of the first and third plays they have studied. The players on defense, although unaware of the play about to be attempted, must unhesitatingly come up with a proper response if they are to squelch the play. This is a drill that should be repeated several times during the season to keep everyone sharp.

(Pages 147–48)

Lesson Objective: To teach and drill the delayed triple steal play.

Drill or Method of Instruction: Important to the success of this play is timing on the part of the runners at first and third. Consequently, it is crucial that the coach spend sufficient time detailing every movement for each runner. It must also be emphasized that in this drill, the defense will often respond perfectly to get the man at the plate. But that will usually happen for one reason—they know what to expect and how to respond! Defenses in game situations will usually be caught totally unaware and will take that crucial extra second to react, and that is all it takes for the play to work successfully. The drill itself is performed like many of the others described here. A defense is placed on the infield while the offensive players rotate as runners at all three bases. It is very important that the coach praise the offensive players whenever they perform their roles with perfect timing, regardless of the outcome of the play at the plate. No one maintains that the play lacks risk or that all runners will find themselves safe despite a perfect response from the defense. But like so many of the other plays described, it is the daring, the alertness, the quickness, and the aggressiveness of the offense, combined with the possibly unprepared state of the defense, that will spell *success* in so many of these efforts.

Appendix

THE HOME-TO-FIRST BASEBALL SPRINT ANALYSIS

[Answer: YES, NO, or S (to indicate sometimes or somewhat)]

	Name	Name

The Start

Station A:

1. The first step after the swing is made with the back foot. ___ ___

Station B:

2. The first few steps are short and choppy. ___ ___

3. The body leans forward rather than upright during the first few steps. ___ ___

The Straightaway

Station C:

4. The eyes are straight ahead on the base, not down. ___ ___

5. The facial muscles are relaxed, not tense with furrows and wrinkles. ___ ___

6. The head remains relatively still without any bobbing or flopping action. ___ ___

Station D:

7. There is a bend of approximately 90 degrees at the elbow. ___ ___

8. The fingers are slightly curled, not wide open nor made into a tight fist. ___ ___

9. The arm swinging never extends beyond the shoulder or below the hips. ___ ___

182

10. The elbows remain close to the side, keeping the arms
    near parallel.
    The hands never extend beyond the center line of the
    chest.
    The shoulders are kept squared to the direction being run.

Station E: 11. The chest extends outward.

Station F: 12. The body leans as a whole, not just from the waist.
           13. The knees lift almost parallel to the ground.
           14. A full extension of the lower leg occurs after the knee
               reaches its maximum height.

Station G: 15. The running is done on the toes.

Station H: 16. The toes point straight ahead, never outward nor inward.
           17. Using a tape measure, determine the length of the stride
               (toe-to-toe) in inches. The stride length should be very
               close to the player's height in inches.

The Arrival
Station I: 18. The base is touched.
           19. The base is touched on the near 4 inches, not in the center
               or far end.
           20. The runner runs through the base rather than leaping for
               it or slowing down as the last step is taken.
           21. The runner stops gradually, not too quickly (to prevent
               possible injury).

183

22. The runner runs only a moderate distance beyond the bag, not too far (which could prevent an advancement if a wild throw were made). _____

23. The runner glances slightly to the right after passing the bag (to spot an overthrow). _____

LEFT-HANDED PITCHER

Baserunning Scouting Form

DATE: _____ TEAM: _____

PITCHER: _____ # _____ (Left-Hander) CHARTER: _____

1. *PITCHING DELIVERY TIME TO*
   THE PLATE: From the windup _____
   From the stretch _____

2. SINGLE RUNNER ON FIRST

As the left-hander was beginning his kick, he:

Inn.	LOOKED TO 1st AND THEN THREW HOME	LOOKED TO 1st AND THEN THREW TO 1st	LOOKED TO HOME AND THEN THREW TO HOME	LOOKED TO HOME AND THEN THREW TO 1st	BEFORE KICKING, HE STEPPED OFF THE RUBBER AND THREW TO 1st

/ = a pitch, or a pickoff attempt that does not involve the 1st baseman moving in.

X = a pickoff attempt that does involve the 1st baseman moving in from behind the runner.

Ø or ⊗ = a successful pickoff

3. SINGLE RUNNER ON SECOND (also 1st & 2nd)

a. NUMBER OF LOOKS:

Inn.	ZERO	ONE	TWO	THREE +

b. PICKOFF ATTEMPTS:

Inn.	CLOCKWISE TURN	COUNTERCLOCKWISE TURN	JOHNNY SAIN TURN *

/ = Unsuccessful
Ø = Successful

* = a kick followed by a counterclockwise turn while in contact with the rubber.

186

RIGHT-HANDED PITCHER

Baserunning Scouting Form

DATE: _____ TEAM: _____
PITCHER: _____ # _____ (Right-Hander) CHARTER: _____

1. *PITCHING DELIVERY TIME*
   TO THE PLATE: From the windup _____
   From the stretch _____

2. *SINGLE RUNNER ON FIRST*
a. NUMBER OF LOOKS: Inn.

	ZERO	ONE	TWO	THREE +

b. PICKOFF ATTEMPTS:

Inn.	OFF RUBBER	MOVING ONTO RUBBER	GOING UP	AT TOP	COMING DOWN	FROM SET	SETS, STEPS OFF, THROWS

/ = Unsuccessful
X = Unsuccessful, & with the 1B moving in

Ø or ⊗ = Successful

---

3. *SINGLE RUNNER ON SECOND* (also 1st & 2nd)

a. NUMBER OF LOOKS:

Inn.	ZERO	ONE	TWO	THREE +

b. PICKOFF ATTEMPTS:

Inn.	CLOCKWISE TURN	COUNTERCLOCKWISE TURN	JOHNNY SAIN TURN *

/ = Unsuccessful
Ø = Successful

* = a kick followed by a counterclockwise turn while in contact with the rubber.

189

CHARTER
RIGHT-HANDED PITCHERS' PICKOFF MOVES TO FIRST BASE
ANALYSIS SHEET

Right-Handed Pitchers

Directions:

Indicate "YES" for a
telltale characteristic

Indicate "NO" for a
nonexistent or
insignificant
characteristic

Circle the most obvious
"YES" characteristic

HEELS									
HEAD AND CAP									
LEFT SHOULDER									

BODY LEAN			
RIGHT KNEE			
LEFT KNEE			
LEFT ELBOW			

HEELS : Write "YES" if the left heel is first lifted on a pitch while the right heel is first lifted on a pickoff attempt.

HEELS AND CAP: Write "YES" if the pitcher fails to give the runner multiple looks before throwing home or if, in throwing to first, he fails to look first away from the runner before returning there with the throw.

LEFT SHOULDER: Write "YES" if the difference between the pitcher's shoulder turn inward (on a pitch) and outward (on a pickoff) is very obvious.

BODY LEAN: Write "YES" if, on a pitch, the pitcher's whole body begins to lean toward the plate because of his hurry to get rid of the ball.

RIGHT KNEE: Write "YES" if the difference between the pitcher's right knee bending (on a pitch) and his right knee stiffening (on a pickoff) is very obvious.

LEFT KNEE: Write "YES" if the difference between the pitcher's left knee bending (on a pitch) and his left knee stiffening (on a pickoff) is very obvious.

LEFT ELBOW: Write "YES" if the pitcher is very obvious in moving his left elbow in and/or up (on a pitch) as opposed to an outward turn (on a pickoff).

LEFT-HANDED PITCHERS' PICKOFF MOVES TO FIRST BASE ANALYSIS SHEET

Left-Handed Pitchers

Directions:

After reading the characteristic descriptions below and on the opposite side, do the following:

Indicate "YES" for a telltale characteristic.

Indicate "NO" for a nonexistent or insignificant characteristic.

Circle the most obvious "YES" characteristic.

Head direction						
Upraised chin/arched or uneven chest						
Leg kick height						
Body lean (to home on a pitch or to 1st on a pickoff)						
Breaking the plane of the rubber						
Sole of the right foot						

Right knee								
Right inner thigh (leg cap)								
Consistent looker								

Characteristic Descriptions

Head direction: Write "YES-S" if the pitcher, on his kick, is *consistently* seen looking in the *same* direction where he eventually throws the ball.

Write "YES-O" if the pitcher, on his kick, is *consistently* seen looking in the *opposite* direction where he eventually throws the ball.

Upraised chin/arched or uneven chest: Write "YES" if the pitcher raises his chin and/or arches his chest and/or assumes an uneven chest and/or assumes an uneven chest position with his left elbow tucked back and in on his pickoff move, but fails to do this with his pitches.

Leg-kick height: Write "YES-H" if there is a noticeably *higher* leg kick when the pitcher throws to first than when he pitches home.

Write "YES-L" if there is a noticeably *lower* leg kick when the pitcher throws to first than when he pitches home.

Body lean: Write "YES-H" if the pitcher is consistently observed leaning toward the plate when he is beginning his kick and eventual pitch home.

Write "YES-F" if the pitcher is consistently observed leaning toward first on his pickoff attempt even before his leg kick reaches its maximum height.

193

Breaking the plane of the rubber: Write "YES" if the pitcher's right leg is consistently seen breaking the plane of the rubber on pitches to the plate.

Sole of the right foot: Write "YES-S" if the pitcher is consistent in showing the *sole* of his right foot at the top of his kick when going home, but showing the instep when going to first.

Write "YES-I" if the pitcher is consistent in showing the *instep* of his foot at the top of his kick when going home, but showing the sole when coming to first.

Right knee: Write "YES-U" if the pitcher consistently turns his right knee inward (without breaking the plane of the rubber) when pitching home, but kicks straight *up* on his pickoffs.

Write "YES-I" if the pitcher consistently turns his right knee *inward* (without breaking the plane of the rubber) when attempting a pickoff, but kicks straight up on his pitches to the plate.

Right inner thigh (leg gap): Write "YES" if, at the top of a pitcher's kick, his right inner thigh is not visible on his pitches, but is visible on his pickoffs due to an extended lateral leg movement toward the first-base dugout.

Consistent looker: Write "YES" if the pitcher consistently looks at the runner while kicking, whether resulting in a pickoff or pitch. In addition, on his pitches, he'll eventually turn his eyes to the plate and pitch. However, on his pickoff, he'll momentarily tilt his head downward as he turns it from the runner, but will then turn his head back to the runner as his pickoff throw is made.

INDEX